THE SERIOUS GARDENER™

ROCK

GARDENS

THE SERIOUS GARDENER™

ROCK GARDENS

THE NEW YORK BOTANICAL GARDEN

TEXT BY
ANNE HALPIN
WITH
ROBERT BARTOLOMEI
MASTER GARDENER

FOREWORD BY
GREGORY LONG
SERIES EDITOR:
TOM CHRISTOPHER

CLARKSON POTTER/PUBLISHERS
NEW YORK

Copyright © 1997 by The New York Botanical Garden

Published by Clarkson N. Potter, Inc., 201 East 50th Street, New York, New York 10022. Member of the Crown Publishing Group.

Random House, Inc. New York, Toronto, London, Sydney, Auckland
http://www.randomhouse.com/

THE SERIOUS GARDENER, CLARKSON POTTER, POTTER, and colophon are trademarks of Clarkson N. Potter, Inc.

Printed in China
Design by Peter Bradford and Danielle Whiteson

Library of Congress Cataloging-in-Publication Data is available upon request.

ISBN 0-609-80087-6
10 9 8 7 6 5 4 3 2 1
First Edition

CONTENTS

FOREWORD

T he Rock Garden at The New York Botanical Garden was created in the 1930s. Situated in a shallow valley between our first-growth forest and the Native Plant Garden, the Rock Garden is one of the most beautiful and captivating places among all our historical landscapes and gardens. The curator of the Rock Garden is Robert Bartolomei, one of the most distinguished members of our horticultural staff. Robert is a *museum* curator in the sense that this is a collection of rock and alpine plants displayed for purposes of public education, and he is a *gardener* because he and his small team are charged with growing the plants and making the garden beautiful.

Robert has been working on this major rock garden since 1988. He has completely remade the garden, repositioning the rocks, restoring the waterfall and stream, remaking the beds, creating new soil and planting media, and rebuilding the plant collection by propagation and acquisition. It is now restored to its position as one of the most important public rock gardens in the world, and it's a marvelous place to visit, especially if you are eager to learn about this challenging kind of horticulture.

During the course of the restoration, Robert has become a great expert on rock plants and their needs, as well as the design of rock gardens. It is fascinating to know that Robert was a generalist in horticulture eight years ago, actually a professional with a particular interest in herbaceous perennials. He learned about rock gardening in order to respond to his new assignment, just as we hope our readers will want

In the alpine meadow planting of the T. H. Everett Rock Garden, plants are tightly massed to form a solid ground cover. Columbines and helcheras flower in June.

to learn from him what may be for them a new kind of gardening.

In publishing our new "Serious Gardener" books, we at NYBG hope to reach an audience of gardeners thinking about new directions in horticulture. In the past, our institutional expertise has been made available to students in our major continuing education program, to people attending lectures here or traveling with our study tours, or to garden visitors in New York. Now through these guides, we are becoming a museum without walls (or perhaps better, without fences), and we hope to be of use to many new friends who live and garden all across the country.

This book is an introduction to rock gardening, but it is also a sophisticated guide to help you make a new kind of garden—whether you have a wild and rocky site or just a few stone steps in need of planting. Robert is sharing with all of us the techniques and the taste that he and his colleagues have employed to make our rock garden here at NYBG such a wonderful place.

I think readers will be surprised and fascinated to learn how timely this intensely traditional field of gardening is. Long before the invention of "natural gardening," rock gardeners were growing their plants in habitats; they understood that natural elements such as rocks had a role not just in design but in the health of the plants; and when rock gardeners spread their gravel mulches, they strived to make the broken stone look like natural deposits. Gardeners, as a whole, are just beginning to understand the role ecology should play in shaping their craft; rock gardeners have decades of experience to share.

What rock gardeners have long known is at last becoming the horticultural mainstream. When you have read this book and thought about the tiny bulbs, crevice plants, and self-sowing plants described by Robert Bartolomei and Anne Halpin, I think you will want at least a small collection of rock plants for yourself. And when you have realized how nice a ledge bed or two would look in front of your woodland edge, I suspect you will be spending more time with your drabas than with your delphiniums!

Gregory Long, President, The New York Botanical Garden

Helleborus niger Officinarum
Ellebore noir usuel

INTRODUCTION

Rock gardens are often described as the realm of the plant obsessed. Indeed, a rock garden is arguably the best possible solution for gardeners whose love of plants can hardly be contained in the area they have available for gardening.

Rock gardens have been part of horticulture since the late 19th century. In the 1920s a rock garden mania seized Great Britain and, as so many gardening styles do, made its way across the Atlantic to take root in the United States. Although many people still think of rock gardens as a peculiarly Victorian pastime, contemporary gardeners will find them surprisingly relevant for today's space restrictions, environmental consciousness, and sophistication.

With the steady contraction in the size of the average yard, many gardeners today do not have the luxury of plenty of space. Our gardens, as often as not, must be tucked into quarter-acre lots or postage-stamp-sized tracts, in whatever space is not already taken up by the house or the garage, the toolshed or the swing set. For gardeners faced with limitations of space, a rock garden offers an opportunity to indulge a passion for plants without the benefit of acres of land.

A fascination with wildflowers is another avenue by which a gardener may come to rock gardening. Many rock garden plants are wildflowers in the sense that they are grown in the garden in their "unimproved" species form. While not all the best plants for American rock gardens are native to this country, most of them still have the delicate, unassuming look and the tough constitution of plants found in the wild. They are quietly beautiful rather than flashy. This is not to say that rock garden plants lack color. To the contrary, many rock plants bloom lavishly despite their diminutive size.

The ideal site for a rock garden is, of course, one that is already rocky, and a homeowner with a property that might otherwise be considered a challenge can create a beautiful landscape without going to the expense of hauling away boulders. Land that is uneven and rocky or tucked up against a ledge or outcrop almost demands a rock garden.

A garden for plant lovers. Practicalities aside, rock gardens are first and foremost about plants. Rock gardening is for gardeners who simply love plants, who become fascinated by their subtle differences of form and habit, beguiled by the beauties of petal and leaf, enthralled by each unique combination of texture and shape. For gardeners drawn to the exquisite charm of small plants, for whom big gardens of boldly shaped and intensely colored plants seem garish and strident, the dainty appearance of rock garden plants is the height of perfection.

A garden built around plants need not look like a haphazard collection, either. Even if the rock garden is born of a fever of plant obsession, it can still be aesthetically pleasing. Good design makes the difference. The rock garden at The New York Botanical Garden combines an interesting assortment of plants in a carefully composed, visually pleasing landscape.

The T. H. Everett Rock Garden. The NYBG's rock garden was designed by Thomas H. Everett, the NYBG's former director of horticulture. At 2½ acres the T. H. Everett Rock Garden is one of the largest public rock gardens in North America. Beginning in 1934, horses and manpower were used to haul huge rocks into the garden to create ledges and outcrops, a waterfall, and a stream. The rocks were carefully organized and positioned to give the appearance of natural geological formations jutting from the soil. The goal was to balance as extensive a collection of rock garden plants as possible with the aesthetic requirements of a landscape garden.

Restoration of the rock garden. Robert Bartolomei, the current curator of the T. H. Everett Rock Garden, took over management of the garden in the spring of 1988. He began to uncover Everett's original design, to correct any structural problems that had developed with the passage of time, and to enhance the garden with new plantings. The garden's structure was still quite beautiful, but after 50 years some areas had experienced considerable erosion and had to be rebuilt, and some of the rocks had shifted out of position. A major problem was that many of the larger woody plants had become overgrown, obscuring views of the overall landscape. Several large conifers and shrubs that could not be pruned had to be removed. Some of the trees intended to provide shade in the woodland area of the garden had died, and many of the delicate plants that had once flourished in their shade failed to survive when exposed to the strong sun.

The passage of time in the garden had, however, also brought great rewards. A rare rhododendron relative from Japan, *Enkianthus perulatus,* with creamy white spring flowers and fiery fall color, planted in the original garden has matured to become the largest specimen of its kind in North America. Several native mountain laurels have grown to an imposing 15 feet, forming an impressive backdrop for parts of the garden.

When the overgrown plants were removed, Everett's basic rockwork was still intact. But although much of the underlying structure of the garden looks much as it did in 1934, many of the plantings have changed. By 1988 only scattered evidence remained of the original plantings, so Bartolomei set out to design new ones for the garden, aiming to balance as extensive a collection of rock garden plants as possible with the aesthetic requirements of a landscape garden in the

Robert Bartolomei's first concern was to restore the original design of the T. H. Everett Rock Garden—50 years of erosion had left many areas in need of a complete rebuilding.

tradition of the great rock gardens created in the early 20th century. One of Robert Bartolomei's goals is to include in the garden a model of each of the major elements that have become traditional in rock gardens, to expose the public to many facets of this very complex form of gardening. This multipurpose approach means that home gardeners and professionals who are interested in rock gardens can use the garden as a sort of living catalog of rock plants, maintained at a high level of horticultural skill. But even casual visitors can appreciate the garden simply for its beauty and for its interpretation of an alpine landscape in a garden setting.

This is an important part of what makes this landscape useful to the home gardener. Many European botanical gardens contain only plants as they are found in the wild, arranged in groups by geographi-

Dogwoods and azaleas are reflected in the pond at the T. H. Everett Rock Garden. Bold foliage of Ligularia dentata *accompanies the globeflowers* (Trollius europaeus) *and ferns.*

cal origin, but the Everett garden includes a combination of natural species and cultivated varieties.

A TOUR OF THE GARDEN

The T. H. Everett Rock Garden was designed to take advantage of a slight increase in grade so that a stroll through it is like taking a journey up a miniature mountainside. First, the visitor passes by a small pond that is below the level of the path. Then the path leads through a woodland area representing the type of forest found at lower elevations on a mountainside. Next, the garden path reveals an often large area called the alpine glade, which features alpine plants. As the garden mimics the ascent to alpine heights, the scale of many of the plants becomes smaller, as it does at higher and higher mountain elevations.

With the sandbed in the foreground and the woodland in the back, the features of the T. H. Everett Rock Garden integrate naturally into the general landscape of The New York Botanical Garden.

From the center of the glade, a look back reveals a long view over a neighboring meadow that enhances the illusion of elevation.

Each part of the garden suggests features appropriate to the corresponding elevation on an actual mountain. Re-creating all the conditions present in the native habitats would be impossible, so the planting areas are not true habitats. They are specialized beds that provide the conditions the plants need to survive in this low-altitude environment.

The adaptations of the plants to their high altitude habitats must be understood in order to provide a garden environment in which rock plants can thrive. The rock gardener must compensate for the lower altitude, higher summer temperatures, higher humidity, and other conditions different from those present in the plants' natural habitats.

Aquilegia species interbreed freely. These growing together in the alpine meadow of the T. H. Everett Rock Garden, allowed to self-sow, show a wide range of characters.

The scree bed. One feature of the Everett rock garden, and many other rock gardens, is an example of such compensation. A natural scree is an area of loose rocks and stones at the bottom of a slope, often deposited there by a landslide. Natural screes are not stable; they shift over time, becoming deeper or more shallow. In the Everett garden the scree bed is a deep, gravelly bed containing relatively little soil and humus, which must be stabilized so the stones stay in place and plants are not dislodged. Most of the species grown in the scree bed at the Everett garden do not inhabit screes in nature. But the scree bed provides the best garden environment for those plants' survival.

Other features. In addition to the scree bed the Everett garden features an area of rock crevices, a sand bed, an acid heath bed, an "alpine meadow," and moist, boggy areas along the pond and stream. The garden also includes a moraine bed, which is essentially a scree area with water flowing below it. In nature the moraine is a true geological remnant of a retreating or passing glacier; the flowing water is the result of ice melting from the glacier's edge. To counterfeit such a habitat in a garden is extra-

More than 100 species of small alpines and rock plants from around the world thrive together in the gravelly soil of the scree bed at the T. H. Everett Rock Garden.

ordinarily difficult; to create moraine bed is beyond the resources of most home gardeners. Since most of the plants grown in the moraine will grow well in a scree bed, the moraine garden is not included in this book.

A host of different habitats are found within the T. H. Everett Rock Garden, including this waterfall and the boggy streamside with its bouquet of yellow irises.

USING THIS BOOK

As a guide to the essentials of rock gardening, this book draws on the knowledge and insight of Robert Bartolomei and the staff of the T. H. Everett Rock Garden. **Chapter 1** presents the basic concepts involved in creating a rock garden: what a rock garden actually is, what kinds of plants belong in a rock garden, and why a love of plants and a willingness to experiment with them is essential to a rock gardener's success.

Chapter 2 defines and explains different kinds of rock plantings suited to a home garden setting, such as ledges, rock crevices, screes, sand beds, alpine meadows, and woodlands and other shady sites. This chapter also offers regional perspectives from several consummate rock gardeners in various parts of the country.

Chapter 3 describes the basics of designing, building, and planting a rock garden, including how to choose a suitable site, how to work with rocks and stone, how to amend garden soil to make an ideal growing medium, and how to plan for paths and access to plants.

The final stage of garden design—choosing plants—can be the most fun, and this topic is also addressed in chapter 3. Dwarf conifers and shrubs provide the basic structure of the plantings, with color and mass supplied by ground-cover and mat plants, bulbs, larger specimen plants, crevice plants, and plants that self-sow.

Chapter 4 covers necessary garden maintenance: planting, fertilizing, watering, weeding, mulching, deadheading, and pruning, as well as collecting and saving seeds to start new plants for next year's garden, and preparing the garden for winter.

Chapter 5 profiles a selection of some of the best rock garden plants, which are well suited to a variety of rock garden situations.

The Appendixes provide resources for gardeners interested in expanding their knowledge about and enjoyment of rock gardening.

If you are an experienced gardener but new to rock gardening, the ideas and tips on technique shared by master gardener Robert Bartolomei should be inspiring. If you are already a proficient rock gardener, we hope you will discover some fresh perspectives, novel approaches, and new plants to grow.

Hardy cacti—Opuntia *and* Echinocereus—*flourish in this Connecticut rock garden, offering a fine example of how rock gardeners are experimenting with plants and exploring new concepts as they adapt this traditional type of garden to new situations.*

1

THE ROCK GARDEN DEFINED

Not every garden requires homework in addition to hard work, but every would-be rock gardener needs to have a clear understanding of just what a rock garden is. Fundamentally, a rock garden is a place where small plants are cultivated in a rocky setting, but not just any assortment of plants, not just any rocks, and not just any soil. A garden in which traditional bed and border plants or annuals are grown in ordinary garden soil with rocks and boulders strewn about for aesthetic appeal is not a true rock garden but what the Victorians dubbed a "rockery." A true rock garden provides special growing conditions and accommodates a carefully selected group of plants suited to those conditions.

Rock gardening as we know it began in the mid-19th century, when English gardeners started creating special garden environments in which to cultivate plants collected all over the world. Tropical exotics found a home in heated and humidified conservatories; mountain-dwelling plants from Europe—called "alpine" for obvious reasons—gave rise to the earliest rock gardens. Today the designation "alpine" continues to be applied somewhat misleadingly to high-mountain plants from many other regions of the world. Mountain plants were not entirely new to English gardeners—they had cultivated auriculas, for example, since the 16th century. But previously, alpines had been cultivated in pots kept in cold frames or were planted out in mixed flower borders.

Most of the early alpine gardens attempted to imitate the look of actual mountains. Often the re-creations were elaborate: the wealthiest collectors centered theirs around "snowcapped" peaks, meticulously sculpted in miniature.

Early rock gardens were usually located out of view of the house or other structures, to foster an air of wilderness. At first the plants were all from high mountains and rocky places, but gardeners quickly learned that many such plants would not survive lower altitudes and higher temperatures, and they began to introduce other plants into the rock setting. Today every rock garden is unique in its combination of plants, its climate, and its geography.

A true rock garden provides special growing conditions and accommodates a carefully selected group of plants suited to those conditions.

Design. Designing a rock garden is somewhat different from designing a more conventional ornamental planting such as an herbaceous bed or border. Whereas other types of gardens can be almost wholly shaped by aesthetic considerations, a rock garden design is dictated by the cultural needs of the plants. Different areas are constructed not just to please the eye but to provide for the requirements of plants from various habitats. A conventional flower gardener may plan a blue-and-white border; the rock gardener plans a scree bed or an alpine meadow, or both.

As noted in the introduction, rock garden construction is an essay in environmental manipulation. The builder compensates for differences between the plants' high-altitude natural habitat and the conditions found in a lowland garden.

Likewise, in the design process, the days of sculpted peaks are long past. Modern rock gardeners strive to evoke the look of moun-

tainous or hilly terrain, but also to integrate the rock garden into the general garden scheme.

Even if the horticultural imperative is more compelling than the aesthetic one in the rock garden, skillful rock gardeners also compose visually pleasing garden pictures, primarily through the deliberate placing of rocks and plants.

Compact and neat, crowned with creamy flower clusters, this mountain buckwheat (Eriogonum ovalifolium) *from California's Sierra Nevada mountains epitomizes the special appeal of alpines. PRECEDING PAGE: Sometimes natural sites look just as we would like our own rock gardens to. This natural "rock garden" in the Sierra Nevadas is "planted" with penstemons, sage brush, eriogonums, and other wildflowers.*

Rock placement might seem to be a simple matter in naturalistic rock gardens such as NYBG's T. H. Everett Rock Garden, where rocks are arranged to resemble naturally occurring outcrops. Yet although the goal of such a garden is to look "natural," each rock is carefully selected, the distances between rocks calibrated, and the final position of each exactingly manipulated. When rocks are already present on a garden site, they can be left as is or repositioned, or others may be brought in and placed by the gardener. Many rock gardens are located on a pre-existing slope, bank, or mound where drainage is naturally quick, although rock gardens can be created on flat ground as well. But whatever the natural topography of the site, a rock garden generally aims at evoking in some manner a rocky or mountainous terrain.

Plantings. The plantings also define a rock garden. Except for shrubs and conifers, the verticality of a rock garden's design depends on terrain alone—the most distinctive feature of most rock plants is that they hug the ground, to conserve heat and to keep out of the wind. Rock gardens still typically include many "alpines," which commonly have a delicate beauty found in few other types of plants—and which are difficult to grow in any other kind of garden—but many other plants may find their way into the modern rock garden, as long as they share the alpines' cultural needs and their small scale.

WHY A ROCK GARDEN?

There are many reasons rock gardening is so captivating. Many of the plants are seldom seen in ordinary gardens because of their special needs. Alpines and other rock plants are often diminutive, and growing such exquisite miniatures is indefinably appealing. Like precious gems, they combine vivid colors with compact, perfectly turned form. In addition, rock garden plants furnish endless variety.

Some gardeners are drawn to the eye-catching look of gentians, with their dazzling blue blossoms. Other gardeners find themselves taken with the subtleties of eriogonums, or mountain buckwheats of

The rich, brilliant blue trumpets of this spring gentian (Gentiana acaulis), *larger than the plant itself, provide all the explanation needed of why these plants intrigue alpine collectors.*

the western American mountains, with their felted leaves, neat dome shapes, and ball-like rose-tinted flower clusters.

Although most rock plants bloom freely, the plant forms are often as attractive as the flowers. Sempervivums, the well-known hens-and-chickens, for example, boast rosettes of succulent leaves. As they mature, they spread lacy mats of succulent foliage in lovely shades of green, red, purple, or bronze that stand out brilliantly against the rugged rocky setting. Many other kinds of rock plants display an appealing mounded form—rock gardeners refer to these as cushions or "buns."

Rock gardening also offers the thrill of challenge, and a true test of horticultural skill. In the beginning, the mere survival of simple rock plants from one year to the next is exciting. Skilled gardeners can add more choice and hard-to-grow species to their collections, growing some of the most demanding plants from seed. Propagating from seed is the only means of obtaining the real rarities—a particularly desirable species of *Androsace,* for example, or a plant newly discovered in the mountains of China or South America.

The ultimate achievement comes when such a challenging plant not only survives in the home garden but also self-sows there to produce a new generation of "volunteer" seedlings. The secret goal of every gardener is to truly understand nature, and for the plant obsessed, the ability to perceive the needs of complex living things and respond to them so well that they thrive—along with the bragging rights it brings—is the ultimate pleasure.

PRACTICAL BENEFITS

In addition to personal gratifications, there are a number of practical reasons for starting a rock garden.

Space. Next to container gardening, rock gardening suits small spaces best. For a small yard, rock gardening affords the best opportunity to explore many different branches of the plant kingdom without turning the landscape into a jumble. Because the plants are typically compact, alpines, bulbs, perennials, ground covers, shrubs, and even trees can be harmoniously combined within a space a few yards square, without seeming to crowd. Rock gardeners are also connoisseurs of dwarf and miniature forms of familiar garden plants. Miniature bulbs, for example, include such as diminutive *Narcissus* species that grow just 3 inches high. Less common plants are intriguing as well, such as a dwarf species of rhubarb. Probably no other kind of garden allows such richness in a restricted space.

Site. Often the existing conditions on a site are a decisive factor for the would-be gardener. Where the only space available for gardening is filled with boulders or natural rock outcrops, a rock garden may be the only type of garden possible without extensive and costly excavation.

Plant hardiness. Many rock garden plants thrive in tough condi-

Any other kind of gardener would have rejected this rocky slope as too problematic to grow flowers and other plants. But by digging down and exposing the outcrops, a rock gardener created an ideal opportunity for a cascade of white-blossomed Antennaria montana, *pink* Lewisia cotyledon, *and red hybrid sun roses* (Helianthemum).

tions where less sturdy hybrids and garden-variety flowers would fail. Plants from the high mountains and other rocky situations are often tolerant of drought, intense sun, and strong winds. Where drainage is excellent, a rock garden may be the most practical type of landscaping for an exposed location.

Manageable maintenance. Once the garden is constructed and planted, rock plants are undemanding. Little or no time is required for staking and pruning, and the soil does not have to be tilled or dug annually, as it does with an annual or vegetable garden, for example. A rock garden is not a low-maintenance proposition, but it is no more labor-intensive than a conventional flower bed or border, and the labor is not physically challenging once the initial construction has been completed. What a rock garden does demand is the continued interest and involvement of the gardener.

PLANTSMANSHIP AND THE ROCK GARDEN

Rock gardeners come to their passion by many routes, but they all share an endless fascination with plants. As Robert Bartolomei explains, the essence of his craft is experimentation, a continual process of trying new plants, keeping those that succeed and discarding or retrying the ones that fail. Rock gardeners are risk takers; they eschew the easy predictability of impatiens and begonias.

For most rock gardeners, rock gardening is not generally a "designer's" approach to gardening, in which plants are used to paint swaths of color in abstract patterns or to echo the colors of the home's exterior or its indoor furnishings. The act of creating a rock garden involves a close study of the plants themselves and an appreciation of their particular qualities. Rock gardens are built plant by plant, and knowing plants is a great benefit of rock gardening. But to be a true plantsman you not only must be able to identify the species and varieties, you must also know how to grow them.

Visiting plants in nature. The best plantsmen begin by studying how garden plants grow in their natural habitats. Unlike many growers of perennials or roses or vegetables, many rock gardeners feel that

it is important to see growing in the wild the plants they wish to grow in their gardens.

For many rock gardeners, a trip to the mountains was the inspiration for their entry into gardening. Typically, rock gardeners have a strong appreciation of plants in their wild form, and of blossoms without the "improvements" of doubled petals, larger flowers, and expanded color ranges that are so sought after in so many bed and border plants. This gives rock garden plantings an unaffected freshness.

Like other rock gardeners, Robert Bartolomei travels specifically to see rock plants growing in a natural state, to learn what the plants look like in the wild, and to study their habitats. Seeing the plants in the wild helps him understand how it may be used in the Everett rock garden. Not only does the plant in nature achieve its true potential, it also tends to grow with other particular plants—its plant associations.

Because plants' natural habitats have such a determining influ-

Success in growing king of the Alps (Eritrichium nanum), *seen here growing wild in the Dolomites of Italy, belongs to only a handful of gardeners, despite over a century of trying. Some alpine species may never be tamed. PRECEDING PAGE: Experienced rock gardeners would recognize many of the plants that inhabit the limestone peaks and hanging screes of the Dolomites.*

ence on the design of rock gardens, these associations are as important as shape and color when making design decisions. Years of research or vast sums of money are not required, since a rock garden can be made with suitable regional wildflowers instead of alpines, and it can contain more common species as well.

THE ROCK GARDEN ENVIRONMENT

Many rock garden plants come from a rigorous high-mountain climate where the wind is strong, cold, and desiccating. The sun can be intense, too. On clear days it is unfiltered by water vapor in clouds or haze, and above the tree line, shade is scarce, found only in the pockets on the north side of boulders and outcrops and in the crevices of large rocks.

The growing season is brief at high altitudes, and even summer weather is cool compared with that of lowlands. In winter, plants

The limestone bluffs of the Bighorns in Wyoming are rich in American alpine species, including Eritrichium aretioides, *the American "king of the mountains." FOLLOWING PAGE: With its crown nestled into a limestone scree in the Bighorns, Jones columbine* (Aquilegia jonesii) *finds protection from the glaring sun and cool moisture below. [photo credit: Bernard Vetter]*

are often insulated from the intense cold and dryness by a constant deep snow cover.

Drainage is never an issue for plants growing in mountain habitats. The soil is thin and contains little humus to hold moisture deposited by rain, and surface water percolates quickly through the stony, rocky ground. Through the evolutionary process, many alpine plants have developed roots that are designed to reach deep into the ground in search of moisture.

To create a rock garden at a lower elevation, the gardener has somehow to compensate for the differences in the environment. High up in the *Summer heat and humidity encourage rotting. The best solution is a soil mix that is light, stable, and extremely well drained.*

mountains, plants may have only 90 to 100 days of active growth each year. At NYBG, for example, the growing season is about 210 days long, summer weather is often hot and humid, and the air commonly is still.

Limiting nutrients. Some rock gardeners control the growth rate of the plants to compensate for the longer growing season, limiting the amount of nutrients, especially nitrogen, which stimulates growth, and organic matter, which releases nutrients as it decomposes. If encouraged to grow quickly over a longer season, rock plants would soon lose their compact habit and the charm that attracted rock gardeners to them in the first place. Rich soil also promotes the kind of soft growth that is especially prone to winterkill. Striking the right balance between healthy growth and starvation requires experience and careful observation.

Drainage problems. If the soil is too heavy and dense, it becomes waterlogged in summer, which causes plants to rot. Wet soil in winter is just as damaging, for rot begins even more quickly in cold weather, fostered by alternate cycles of freezing and thawing. For many rock plants even the leaves resting on moist soil is enough to cause crown rot. Summer heat and humidity also encourage rotting. The best solution is a soil mix that is light, stable, and extremely well drained.

Competing plants. One theory about rock plants is that many flourish in such seemingly inhospitable conditions because there is so little

Gardeners usually think of Turkey as the home of many of our popular spring bulbs. In recent years, however, plants suitable to rock gardens have been introduced from such areas as the Taurus Mountains.

competition from other plants. In more congenial environments—such as those found in conventional garden beds and borders—other, stronger plants would easily outcompete and overwhelm the smaller rock plants. Some rock plants *will* grow in beds of typical garden soil, as long as the gardener eliminates any competition from weeds and other vigorous plants, but for most rock plants standard garden conditions are fatal.

THE ROLE OF ROCKS

The rocks in a rock garden are decorative, of course, but they serve several horticultural functions as well. Rocks and stones cast shade that helps keep the soil cool, which is beneficial to the rock plant roots. Rocks also help to regulate moisture in the garden, channeling it toward the plant roots deep underground and slowing the evaporation of moisture from the soil and the air immediately around plants. Small

Inhospitable as the rocks may look to a human eye, they offer shade and shelter from the wind to this wild Androsace villosa *in Turkey's Taurus Mountains, and when rain falls, the boulders channel the moisture down to the plants' roots.*

stones and gravel likewise play a part in moisture management. When incorporated into the soil mix, they enhance drainage by allowing water to pass quickly through the upper layers and so keep the plants' crowns dry and safe from rot while providing roots with essential moisture.

In the Everett garden, Robert Bartolomei also uses rocks as barriers to separate distinct growing environments with different soil mixes for plants with differing requirements—in effect, a container garden in the ground. A warmer location on the south side of a rock or the cooler, shadier north side can accommodate plants that favor slightly warmer or cooler conditions.

Finally, on a bank or slope, rocks and stones help hold the soil in place and prevent erosion.

The beauty of rocks. The aesthetic virtues of rocks may be overlooked by a vegetable gardener tilling the soil for seeds, but to the rock gardener, nothing is more beautiful. Artfully placed rocks introduce an element of drama. They form backdrops and color contrasts, supporting and displaying each plant to its best advantage. Rock plants are individuals, and the rock garden treats them as specimens, highlighting the virtues of each rather than blending them together. When they are draped over a ledge or cascade down an outcrop, their softness and delicacy contrast sharply with the rugged strength of the rock.

To achieve the most pleasing design, rocks must be arranged naturally; an ineptly ordered composition may make the garden look like little more than a pile of stones surrounded by plants. Obviously, experience cannot be taught, but useful tips are offered in chapter 3.

WHAT IS A ROCK GARDEN PLANT?

Any small plant that thrives in a rocky environment is potential material for the rock garden. Rock garden plants may be annual or perennial, shrubby or herbaceous, easy to grow or challenging. Good plants for rock gardens include dwarf conifers, small shrubs and trees, ferns, small perennials and wildflowers, ground covers, bulbs, and, of course, alpines.

Classic alpines. Alpines, plants that naturally occur on mountain peaks and meadows above the tree line, are the classic rock garden plants, and they still set the standards for rock garden plants.

Most rock gardeners, for example, limit their herbaceous plantings to species that grow less than a foot tall, and they plant only dwarf conifers of a height of 3 feet or less. This reflects the compact form common to alpines. These are compact because plants with short, closely spaced stems and small leaves are better able to tolerate the intense sunlight and wind of mountain habitats than those with a more open form. Likewise, compact plants are better able to survive the high-mountain winters, enduring the weight of deep snow cover.

Blooming habits. The majority of alpines bloom quickly, generously, and colorfully. That again reflects their harsh heritage: in the wild, they must compete hard to attract the scarce pollinators of their mountain environment and must set seed within the confines of a short growing season. The brief, brilliant burst of blossoms they produce means that most rock gardens reach peak bloom in April, May, and June.

Evolutionary adaptation to alpine conditions has transformed a member of the often weedy bindweed genus (Convolvulus) *into a superb cushion alpine in the Taurus Moutains, Turkey.*

Although gardeners speak of alpines as a single group, in fact the different alpine plants originate in a variety of different ecological niches: rocky outcrops and boulder-strewn fields, crevices and small pockets on ledges and cliff faces, screes or moraines, meadows, or even bogs. The plants from each type of habitat demand a different set of growing conditions if they are to flourish. (These habitats are discussed in chapter 2, and growing conditions are included in the descriptions of individual plants in chapter 5.)

Alpine habitat features. Factors that are common to all alpine habitats (in varying degree) are a rocky terrain and thin, gritty soil; cool summer temperatures; and nearly continuous air movement. Most rock plants are accustomed to bright, unobstructed sunlight, but there are some shade-adapted species as well. Although in the natural habitat the shade would have been provided by boulders, these species will often perform equally well in wooded settings where the ground is stony.

A clumping fescue, maiden pinks (Dianthus deltoides), *and* Aster tongolensis *grow through the ground-covering thymes of the alpine meadow at the T. H. Everett Rock Garden.*

Places like the Beartown Plateau in Montana are often visited by rock gardeners wishing to see alpines in their natural homes. The dramatic scenery as well as the plants are a great source of inspiration.

Shallow, well-drained soils are the norm in most alpine environments, but soils are deeper and somewhat richer in high-mountain meadows, where a variety of grasses, bulbs, and wildflowers flourish. Along streams are even found poorly drained, boggy areas, and there is a small group of rock garden plants specifically adapted to these conditions.

Saxatile or rock plants. Plants from lower elevations that also like to grow in rocky sites are called saxatile or rock plants, and they are often easier to grow in gardens than true alpines. *Phlox subulata,* the moss phlox, for example, long a standard rock garden plant, is native to the lower elevations of eastern North America, where it grows mainly on rocky outcrops. Most rock gardens include both alpine and saxatile plants. In this book, the term "rock plants" refers to plants native to rocky environments of both high and lower elevations.

Bulbs and perennials. In addition to rock plants, it is also possible

On this dry rocky ledge in the T. H. Everett Rock Garden, plants such as Phlox subulata *carpet the garden with color in May. OPPOSITE: A stream brings an added dimension to the rock garden—a waterway may be counterfeited with a swath of gravel, as in the T.H. Everett Rock Garden, above, or created by tapping a nearby spring, as in the Pennsylvanian garden, right.*

to work smaller bulbs and perennials into the rock garden. Of the perennials, spreading and mat-forming types generally fit best. See chapter 5 for information about these and other plants recommended for rock gardens.

Plants must be selected with care, though, or the garden may become merely a rockery and lose its special character. It is best to forgo plants that would grow just as well in a flower bed or border.

Collection from the wild. A final note about rock plants: Although some rock gardeners try to be purists, cultivating only the wild forms of every species, common sense dictates a compromise. Plants collected from the wild have a poor rate of survival in the garden. In addition, since collecting puts additional pressure on wild populations that may already be endangered, environmentally conscious rock gardeners

A rock garden can include not only true alpines but also saxatile plants such as this moss pink (Phlox subulata), *an American wildflower native to rocky habitats at lower elevations.*

commonly rely on specimens grown from wild collected seed or selected forms of the plants. Selected forms are no longer considered "wild," having been bred from generations of garden survivors, but these cultivated plants preserve the look of their wild ancestors, even if they have adopted fancy names and domesticated habits.

SOURCES OF PLANTS

Many plants for rock gardens can be found at garden centers and nurseries, along with saxatile plants such as basket-of-gold (*Aurinia saxatilis*) and moss phlox (*Phlox subulata*), which are also used in beds and borders. A far richer source of rock garden plants is specialty nurseries. Gardeners who are willing to raise their own plants from seeds should consider joining the North American Rock Garden Society.

The perennial candy tuft (Iberis sempervirens), *with its bright white flowers and dark green foliage, is an evergreen shrublet that is native to Spain.*

Membership in a local chapter of the North American Rock Garden Society also puts the gardener in touch with other enthusiasts, and in the end, that may be the best source of cuttings, seeds, and divisions. Rock gardening can be very social; rock gardeners love to get together, not only to swap seeds and plants but also to share information with kindred spirits and to exchange travel stories. Attending one of the society's regional or national meetings can extend this circle of gardening friends far beyond your region, even beyond national borders. Over time, your rock garden will take on an international flavor as it comes to include species from all over the world.

See Appendix A for listings of some good sources of plants and seeds. Membership information for rock garden groups may also be found there.

Yellow-blossomed basket-of-gold (Aurinia saxatilis) *and rosy-flowered moss pink* (Phlox subulata) *are two common perennials that lend themselves to the rock garden as well as the border.*

Throughout this book plants are referred to primarily by their botanical names. Although common names are often colorful and are more familiar to many gardeners, they can also be confusing. Common names differ from place to place, and there are some very different plants that share the same common names. Botanical names, although subject to occasional revision and a certain amount of argument, are a more precise means of identifying plants.

Use of botanical names is especially important in rock gardening because the plants originate from all over the world and the system of Latin botanical nomenclature is internationally recognized and uniform. Any two gardeners can understand which plant is called *Aquilegia flabellata,* whereas one might call the plant by the common name fanleaf columbine while the other knows it as Japanese columbine. Only the use of botanical names can guarantee clear communication, and that the plant received from a mail-order nursery or seed exchange is the one that was ordered.

The taller flowering plants of the meadow in the T. H. Everett Rock Garden emerge from low tufts or rosettes of foliage. The stalks are cut back after flowering to maintain a low ground cover.

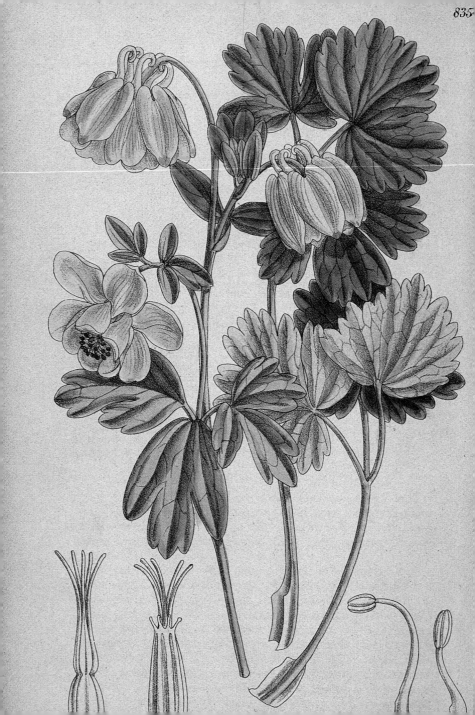

2

ROCK GARDEN
FEATURES

A lthough it would be stretching the truth to call it a revolution, the shift in rock garden design—away from replication of the mountainside and toward a naturalistic integration of the rock garden into the existing landscape—has dramatically altered the role of the rock garden in horticulture. Drawn by the new opportunities this change has created, American rock gardeners are developing their own themes as they incorporate regionally adapted plants into rock gardens. Although traditional elements of the rock garden are outlined below, would-be rock gardeners should feel free to interpret these in their own personal style.

Nevertheless, the traditional elements deserve close study because they are the results of a century of experimentation and polishing. Each one offers a most effective device for growing a different group of rock plants, while at the same time offering a different design option. By choosing among them you can assemble a garden suited to a variety of sites. Depending on the space available and the terrain, a garden may be constructed from one feature or several in combination.

LEDGES

Rocks set into the face of a slope in a sort of natural-looking terraced arrangement are known to rock gardeners as ledges. Ledges offer a number of advantages. In a steeply sloping garden, ledges, either natural or man-made, secure the soil that would otherwise erode downhill. Ledges can also be used to face the opposing banks along a path or driveway; in such a situation they can transform a very artificial type of landscape feature into a natural-looking valley, and a fine rock garden.

As the main flush of May-flowering rock plants winds down, taller plants such as the purple foxgloves, salvias, feverfews, and penstemons continue the colorful display in the T. H. Everett Rock Garden.

Construction. Though they are most easily constructed from large rocks set deep into the slope face, they may also be pieced together from smaller rocks set side by side with their top at the same height so that they appear to be of a single piece. Planting mat-forming species into the joint will help mask the deception. In general, constructing a convincing ledge is easier than creating a natural-looking outcrop or an aesthetically pleasing dry wall, which makes ledges ideal for first-time rock gardeners. If the rocks in the ledge are angled into the slope with their bases pointing downward, then the upper edges of the exposed rock will trap rainwater as it runs down the slope, directing this moisture back into the soil around the plant roots. What's more, ledges are good not only for growing plants, but also for displaying them. With a carefully orchestrated series of ledges, the rock garden can become dramatic, sweeping landscape.

Other advantages. Ledges offer a number of other advantages. Constructing a ledge is simpler than making an artificial outcrop or a dry-laid stone wall, and it requires the placement of fewer—though larger—rocks, which makes ledges ideal for the first-time rock gardener. Ledges also provide excellent showcases for plants, because they raise the plants up the slope, above ground level, closer to eye level.

In addition, ledges afford a wealth of horticultural possibilities, since their many niches can accommodate most of the plants the average rock gardener might want to grow. Mat-forming plants can spread over the pockets of soil they create; mounded plants will flourish there, too. For real drama, trailing plants may be draped over the rocks and allowed to spill over the edges.

OUTCROPS

Outcrops are rock formations that jut out of the ground, and they offer the simplest means of creating a rock garden on a flat site. They may occur naturally in the garden, but they may also be constructed. Installing a convincing artificial outcrop is a challenge, but when it is

The foliage of the Christmas rose (Helleborus niger) *emerges from a mat of* Campanula fenestrellata *on this constructed outcrop. FOLLOWING PAGE: This property in Hastings, New York, with its natural outcrops, proved to be the perfect site to create a rock garden.*

skillfully done, as in the Everett garden at the NYBG, the result may be nearly indistinguishable from a natural outcrop.

The easiest method is to heap up a berm, or mound, of rock garden soil mix and then set a large rock or carefully fitted combination of rocks into its face. The most natural effect will be achieved by tilting the angle of the rock's strata so that the whole arrangement appears to thrust up out of the ground, as if shifted by the upheavals of nature. If the result is not effective, it is relatively easy to tear apart the outcrop and begin again.

ROCK CREVICES

In nature, crevices run through most rocky outcrops, supporting a broad range of rock plants. In the garden, crevices can be constructed by joining rocks closely together and then filling the space in between with soil. The size of the rocks depend on the materials available and should be in scale with the rest of the garden. Small rocks can serve as well as large. But to provide an adequate home for plants, a crevice must be deep; a shallow niche with its small pocket of soil does not allow for sufficient root growth. A properly constructed crevice is a fissure that runs between the rocks all the way to the soil beneath them, allowing plant roots to extend into the earth below. The crevice should be no wider than ½ inch, however, to discourage invasion by weeds.

Many European rock gardens are constructed from a large quantity of small rocks to create as many crevices as possible. These must be skillfully arranged if the result is not to look like a rock pile, but the many seams do create a wealth of crevices. This type of construction is less common in the United States, however, not only because of its difficulty but also because of the time and expense involved in acquiring and installing such a large quantity of stone.

Crevice advantages. A crevice is the most congenial home for many rock plants. The crown of the plant stays dry because it rests on the rock, and the position of the plant—isolated from other plants and jutting out from the surrounding rocks—allows for maximum air circulation around the top growth. The threat of crown rot is thus decreased, and even in hot weather the roots of the plant remain cool.

The best crevice plants. Plants that are especially well adapted to crevices are those with long, stringy roots that can reach down deeply to underlying soil. Two plants that Bartolomei has found to be well suited to crevices are *Ramonda myconi* and *Lewisia cotyledon*. Other good plants for crevices are the saxifrages, which have extensive but very fine roots that coat the rock surfaces of the crevices with a tissue-paper–like mat. Most crevice plants will also grow in other types of garden situations, but they look especially at home in a crevice.

There are some plants, however, that do not take kindly to crevices. These include those mat-forming species such as the veronicas whose stems need to keep rooting into the soil as they spread.

Dry stone wall. If you admire crevice plants but do not want to go to the trouble of installing the large boulders required by a naturalistic setting, Bartolomei suggests an alternative. You can instead build a "dry" stone wall—a wall in which the stones are simply set one on top

For the gardener who feels unequal to Nature in arranging stones in a pleasing design, a dry wall offers a handsome and very effective device for growing and displaying rock plants.

of the other brickwork style and the joints filled with soil rather than mortared. Such a wall may be built up against the foot of a slope or used to enclose a raised bed. The raised bed in particular offers a wealth of planting opportunities: crevice plants fill the joints of the side walls, while the well-drained soil atop the bed may be used for other sorts of rock plants and small shrubs.

Considerations of crevice gardening. Crevice gardening requires some special techniques. Because the plants must fit their roots to the narrow space, it is best to use small young specimens or even just rooted cuttings when planting a crevice. In that way, roots can grow to fit.

It is also essential to check regularly for weeds around and under crevice plants. Pinch out the weed seedlings while they are small. If a weed gains a foothold in a crevice, it is very difficult to remove it without also ripping out the desirable plant and most of the soil in the crevice, too. In Bartolomei's experience, the safest way to deal with such a problem is to take a small paintbrush and paint the weed with a

Dry wall joints between stones are filled with soil, rather than mortar, creating the kind of well-drained but cool, deep soil pockets in which rock plants thrive.

glyphosate herbicide, leaf by leaf. This treatment is slow but effective and should not harm the rock plant. Nor should it affect the garden environment as a whole, since the amount of herbicide used is tiny.

SCREES

In nature, a scree is a sloping area covered with loose stones and rock debris. Usually it occurs at the base of a cliff or steep hill, where stones have been deposited by a landslide. In earlier rock gardens, a scree bed was typically arranged as an area of gravelly soil spilling and fanning out between outcrops of rock as screes do in nature. But rock gardeners today tend to treat a scree as simply a bed with an extra-gravelly soil mix.

Scree beds are probably the most popular feature of rock gardens in the United States. The excellent drainage they afford makes them especially useful in regions where rainfall is high and rock plants would otherwise succumb to crown rot. Another reason for the popularity of scree beds is that they allow the gardener to grow a range of rock plants

As broken stone piles up at the foot of a cliff or steep slope, a natural scree forms, creating a fan of deep, gravelly soil that is especially hospitable to many kinds of rock plants.

without having to go to the trouble and expense of building in stone.

Scree beds may also readily be used in conjunction with other garden features. You might create some planting areas with the standard rock garden soil mix (a blend of equal parts loam, compost, and gravel or coarse sand), while filling others with a scree mix to allow for the cultivation of choice plants.

Drainage. Site a scree bed so water can drain through it quickly. If the site is level or low, or if the underlying soil is dense and heavy with clay, water may collect below the scree bed after heavy rains and cause the plants to rot. To ensure adequate drainage, scree beds should be located in raised areas, such as on a slight rise at the foot of a slope. A raised bed can simply be filled with scree mix, or a series of berms can be built up with the mix; in such a rock garden, there need actually be few rocks.

The rock gardener's artificial scree (such as the one at the T. H. Everett Rock Garden pictured here) reproduces the perfectly drained, gravelly soil of the natural prototype, and is one of the best means of cultivating rot-prone alpines in humid regions such as New York.

If the subsoil is well drained, a scree bed can be laid on level ground. The first step is to excavate the existing soil to a depth of at least a foot. Then loosen the subsoil and chop it into clods (not small bits). Next, spread some of the scree soil mix on top of the loosened subsoil and mix the soils together lightly. In Bartolomei's experience, blending the scree mix into the subsoil too thoroughly reduces the effectiveness of the drainage.

Adjusting for abundant rainfall. In regions such as the eastern United States, where rainfall is abundant, the leaner the scree mix—that is, the more coarse drainage material mixed into it—the better. Where rainfall is less abundant and the garden receives less moisture, the soil mix can contain more loam and humus. In the arid climates of the West and Southwest, a special soil mix for scree beds is largely unnecessary because rainfall is so infrequent.

Exposure. Scree beds, when sited on an unobstructed north- or eastern-facing slope so that they receive some cooling shade in the afternoon, are one of the best places to grow the smaller, choicer, more difficult rock plants. These include many of the classic alpines, such as androsaces, drabas, saponarias, and saxifrages. Plants from more arid climates, such as *Hypericum olympicum,* grow well in scree beds with sunnier exposures.

SAND BEDS

Sand beds have become a popular rock garden feature in recent years, and with good reason. They are easy and quite inexpensive to construct. A sand bed, whether a simple raised bed or a bed directly on the ground, is basically a foot-deep layer of coarse builder's sand with no organic matter or soil added. The absence of organic matter in the sand bed makes it a good growing medium for rock plants that normally succumb to rot in any other kind of soil mix. In high-rainfall areas, Mediterranean plants such as lavender also grow better in a sand bed than in an ordinary garden setting.

Advantages of sand beds. Sand is easy to work with and to maintain. It requires no mixing, and weeds are easy to pull in sand beds. Best of all for northern zones, rock plants are far less prone to frost heaves. (Frost heaving occurs as a result of the alternate freezing and thawing of the soil in wintertime, which can actually push plants up out of the ground.) Frost heaving seldom occurs in a sand bed, because sand does not hold enough moisture to freeze and buckle. Finally, winterkill is much less likely in the extremely well drained conditions of a sand bed. Many rock plants prefer dry conditions in winter and will actually withstand lower temperatures if the area around their roots remains dry. The same plant that fails to survive the winter in an ordinary bed may overwinter without harm a few feet away when its roots are resting in sand.

When installing a sand bed, make the layer of sand no deeper than 1 foot. Sand does not retain nutrients or moisture for plants, so roots must grow through it and into the soil below to nourish the top growth. Small, young plants will have difficulty establishing themselves in deep sand unless additional fertilizer and water are supplied.

Since sand sifts through any gaps and slides away down sloping grades, sand beds are usually built on a level site. For a raised bed, the retaining walls need to be of a solid material such as an earthen berm or mortared brick. For a steeply sloping site, levels must by terraced.

Problems with sand beds. One limiting factor of the sand bed is that it can never be so large that once completed it requires walking on its surface for maintenance. Stepping onto the sand, even to carry out essential gardening chores such as planting or weeding, will disturb this loose substrate. Design the bed so that its center can be reached while standing outside it, or else plan to install paths or steppingstones that will allow access to the interior.

A surprising number of rock plants will thrive in a sand bed, so long as they are somewhat drought tolerant and have deep root systems. Armerias, dianthus, and arenarias are very much at home here. It is also one of the best places to grow *Phlox bifida* (sand phlox).

ALPINE MEADOWS

Sometimes called an alpine lawn, the alpine meadow is as much a style of planting than a particular environment. In nature, alpine meadows are open areas of low grasses, sedges, and flowering plants that flourish between the forest and high alpine zones. They form a nearly solid ground cover, so that when in flower they are a carpet of color.

Meadows as transitions. You can create the effect of an alpine meadow in an open, level or slightly sloping area of the rock garden by planting the area with low-growing bulbs, wildflowers, and/or ground covers. This type of planting is a useful way to integrate the rock garden into the general landscape. As the meadow spreads out around the rocky features of the garden, it provides a gentle transition from mowed lawn to the rugged look of the rockwork.

There are a number of ways to interpret the concept of the alpine meadow. In the Everett garden, the alpine meadow is located on a level spot surrounded by a series of constructed outcrops. In it are planted small spring- and autumn-flowering bulbs such as crocuses and bulb irises in a more or less solid ground cover of thymes, phloxes, and other mat-forming rock plants, with a few taller tufted plants such as columbines used as accents.

Some species plantings. A meadowlike effect can be created by planting more closely together the same species that are also found in screes or other rock garden environments. Take care, though, to select plants carefully so that their size and vigor are suited to the scale of the meadow you are trying to create. For a meadow of only a couple of square yards, for example, *Geranium dalmaticum* would be preferable to the larger Lancaster geranium (*G. sanguineum* var. *striatum*). Although grasses are a natural component of real meadows, it is not wise to include any of the stoloniferous kinds (that is, those that spread by runners) in this type of planting. In fact, an alpine meadow need not include any grasses at all.

WOODLANDS AND OTHER SHADY SITES

Rock gardeners have engaged in a lively debate about whether or not a rocky woodland can legitimately be considered a kind of rock garden, because the plants grown there are usually small woodland plants and wildflowers—such as trilliums, epimediums, and ferns—instead of alpines.

While the cultural needs of woodland plants lie outside the province of this book, it is worth mentioning them if only to remind rock gardeners that they should keep them in their repertoire. Most home rock gardens, at least in temperate regions, include some shady areas. Many properties in the East, Southeast, Midwest, and Northwest have been carved out of forest or woodlands. Especially in areas with hot summers, many gardeners find shade, particularly afternoon shade, very useful in keeping the rock garden cooler. This in turn can be vital to the survival of the plants.

An assortment of brightly colored rock plants tumble down the slopes of this rock garden in Mendenhall, Pennsylvania. Pieris, rhododendrons, and a pink-flowering dogwood in the background indicate this is peak flowering time in May. PRECEDING PAGE: The ferns, forget-me-nots, yellow monkey flowers, and astilbe growing on the banks of the woodland stream provide a lush contrast to the low and compact plants of the alpine glade in the T. H. Everett Rock Garden.

Deep rocks in Nancy Goodwin's shady garden effectively keep hungry rodents away from the bulbs of these species tulips.

One of the toughest environments for rock gardening is the southeastern United States. In the Southeast, the soil is heavy with clay, the air is humid, and summer temperatures are torrid, cooling only slightly overnight. But even in these difficult conditions, rock gardens can thrive. The secret is continual experimentation with plants and ways to manipulate growing conditions.

In North Carolina, for example, Nancy Goodwin has maintained a rock garden at her present home for 15 years, and one part of the garden has existed for many years, possibly since the 19th century. Her rock garden comprises two very different sections. The original, old garden is in the shade, built around existing quartzite rocks of varying sizes that appear to be a natural outcrop. The northern end of this garden receives a fair amount of sun; the southern end is shadier.

The shady garden has proved an ideal place for bulbs; rodents cannot get to them because of all the deep rocks. Species crocuses—both spring and fall types—provide continuous bloom from October to April. Small species tulips, anemones, and trilliums also thrive.

A highlight of the shady garden is the hardy cyclamens, which bloom through much of the year. *Cyclamen purpurascens* graces the garden with rose-pink flowers in summer and is followed in autumn by the blossoms of *C. cilicium* and *C. hederifolium*. In winter, *C. coum* is in bloom, along with *C. repandum* and *C. pseudibericum*.

A newer part of the rock garden, which Nancy Goodwin built herself, is on a flat, sunny site. This section of the garden is a scree bed, the soil mounded up to form hummocks, with sunken paths running through the plantings. Plants in the scree bed grow in a mix of 50 percent clay loam and 50 percent pea gravel and are mulched with 4 inches of pea gravel.

In the sunny garden, armerias thrive for years, along with opuntias, agaves, and the *Androsace* species *carnea, lanuginosa,* and *sarmentosa.*

> *The secret of successful rock gardening in the South is continual experimentation.*

A small sun-loving fern, *Cheilanthes lanosa,* has done well. Lavenders, oreganos, and saturejas also flourish in the sunny, well-drained scree bed. In fact, so many plants do so well that they outgrow the garden after a number of years and have to be moved.

To enable rock plants to grow in the hot, humid climate, the Goodwins add lime to the soil in their gardens in particular spots for plants that need it. They also grow some plants in large scree pots, removing them from the garden entirely. Some scree pots are filled with a mix of equal parts soil and gravel, some have a mix of 40 percent soil and 60 percent gravel, and others contain a lean mix of 20 percent soil and 80 percent stone.

Plants are watered only until they become established, except for the large scree pots, which need water more regularly. Fertilizing varies. Scree plants receive some fertilizer when they are planted, but the shady garden was fertilized in 1995 for the first time in ten years, with an all-purpose organic plant food.

Even more problematic than the soil is the hot, humid, still air in summer. Many plants succumb to the sticky conditions, and the Goodwins experiment continuously. Growing tropicals is not an option, since temperatures regularly plummet to zero in winter and have dipped as low as $-12°$ F.

Nancy Goodwin's advice for beginning gardeners is simple. "Never believe anyone who tells you that you can't grow a plant," she declares. "Try plants in different situations and in different proportions of stone and soil. And don't give up if a plant doesn't survive the first time you plant it. You can expect to kill a particular plant species three times before you write it off," she suggests. "And when you do decide the plant just will not work for you, there are always plenty more to try."

A ROCK GARDEN IN DENVER

Sometimes a gardener comes to rock gardening through necessity as well as preference. Denver's arid climate, says Robert Nold, makes perennial gardening "one long scream of despair." But

"Denver has probably the best climate in the world for growing a variety of alpine plants."

the dry air and brilliant sunshine of the mile-high city make it an ideal place for a rock garden.

Actually, Nold was drawn to rock gardening initially because of his interest in native plants, particularly dryland species. In Colorado, high-mountain plants were all around him. Along the way, though, he has learned that alpines and other rock plants just simply grow better in his garden than do conventional garden plants.

"Denver has probably the best climate in the world for growing a variety of alpine plants, without much need for protection of any kind," he says. It's a tough climate for most kinds of plants, to be sure. Nold describes it as "a Mediterranean climate designed by someone from Minnesota."

Only about 10 inches of rain falls in the course of a year, most of it in summer. Snow is frequent in winter, but it seldom lasts long, melting and drying in 48 hours. The sun is intense, and the wind is strong, often sending gusts up to 100 miles per hour whipping over the land. The average daytime temperature in winter is $50°$ F, with occasional drops to 20 below. "I like to tell people we have zone 8 winters with occasional interludes of zone 4," says Nold.

Denver gets its first taste of spring in January, when the snowdrops bloom. From then until late May or June there are alternate periods of warmth and bitter cold. The warm temperatures in January often lure perennials, broad-leaved evergreens, and other bed and border plants out of dormancy, only to be frozen by a cold snap. But alpines aren't fazed by the severe conditions. "They don't care," says Nold.

Nold grows a variety of classic alpines in troughs, where he can control the growing conditions during bouts of bad weather. The plants grow in ordinary soil (which locally contains a fair amount of clay). They have to be watered daily in summer during dry periods. During spells of wet weather, he must sometimes cover cushion plants with plastic to prevent crown rot, since the soil does retain more moisture than do many rock garden soils.

The troughs are full of classic alpine species—*Eritrichium aretoides;* a number of *Androsace* species, including *A. chamaejasme* ssp. *carinata* (which is native to Pike's Peak), *A. ciliata, A. hedraeantha,* and *A. vandellii;* and several species of *Douglasia,* including *D. laevigata, D. montana,* and *D. nivalis.* "*Polemonium viscosum,* which everybody says is an annual, has lived here for six years in a trough and is very happy," he declares with a sense of satisfaction. There are also lewisias, saxifrages, and other species.

In addition to the troughs, there are seven raised beds in Nold's backyard. To make the beds, he simply mounded up soil 2 feet high and added some rocks gathered from along the roadside. Plants are grouped in the beds according to their moisture needs. One bed is devoted to cacti (Nold grows hundreds of them), particularly the genus *Echinocereus.* Another important genus in this garden is *Acantholimon,* the prickly thrifts, which are native to Turkey and central Asia. The plants form domes of sharp leaves gathered into rosettes. The flowers—mostly pink—bloom on slender wands and are followed by interesting seed heads. Over time the domes of foliage spread, outliving many other kinds of plants. The sunny, dry conditions suit them just fine.

All but one of the raised beds were made with the existing soil, which is,

Though not classic alpine plants, agaves thrive in Nancy Goodwin's sunny garden, and their bursts of foliage help give structure to the overall planting scheme.

according to Nold, "awful. It's someone else's subsoil," he says, the dumpings from another of the builder's projects. Underneath this layer of poor soil, though, lies a richer creek-bottom soil. To grow more traditional garden plants, Nold has to scrape away the top layer so that he can plant in the good soil beneath. But for rock plants the existing soil suffices. "If you don't water it, it's an ideal growing medium for a lot of plants that like dry conditions," he explains.

The one bed that houses difficult-to-grow species is filled with soil made of composted turves. Nold created this through inspired opportunism: when a neighbor down the street removed an old lawn, Nold persuaded him to dump the old sod on his property. This bed's soil may be different, and its plantings distinct, but its appearance still harmonizes with the others: Nold spreads a pea-gravel mulch over all the beds to create a uniform look, as well as to keep the plants cool, and to protect them from neighborhood cats.

As for all rock gardeners, the thrill for Robert Nold lies in the challenge of growing difficult species. His current favorite is the genus *Eritrichium*, possibly the most difficult of all alpines to grow. "They deeply resent humid air," he explains, "and are extremely exacting as to their requirements." One of his greatest achievements was an *Eritrichium aretoides* that flowered for a couple of years. Unfortunately, this same plant subsequently taught him a lesson in the need for consistency: he forgot to water it during a dry spell one summer and the plant died.

But in the rock garden there's always a new challenge to take on, and a new plant to try.

Echinocereus *cacti in full bloom lend a native American flair to this scene in Robert Nold's Denver garden:* Arenaria ledebouriana *spills a drift of white flowers, while* Lallemantia canescens *blossoms in purple and* Helichrysum aureum *bears yellow flowers.*

Many gardeners tend to think of the Northwest as a plant paradise where the climate is mild and moist. But that's actually true only along the Pacific Coast. The rest of the Northwest has a variety of climates. In southern Oregon, where Baldassare Mineo lives, the weather is dry and ideal for rock gardening.

Mineo is the proprietor of Siskiyou Rare Plant Nursery, a premier source of rock garden plants and unusual perennials. His 2-acre rock garden receives less than 20 inches of rain a year, most of it falling from November through April. Normal winter low temperatures are in the low 20s to the upper teens, but they can drop down to zero occasionally, and that's without snow cover. "Normally, we're in the 20s," explains Mineo, "and in a mild winter we can get by with hardly dropping below 25 degrees."

Baldassare Mineo began growing perennials in California 20 years ago and started a small wholesale business there, when, he says, "people didn't really know what perennials were." He started selling to some of the better nurseries, and when American gardeners discovered perennials, his business took off and he needed room to expand. On a trip to Oregon in search of property, he found not just a piece of land he liked but a little business as well—Siskiyou Rare Plant Nursery. He has owned the nursery, which was founded in 1963, since 1978. He moved the business to the 4-acre parcel he had found and began developing the gardens. The nursery has since expanded.

Mineo started rock gardening 17 years ago while he was growing perennials in California. "I do love perennials and border gardening and cottage gardening," he says. But he found himself looking for a style of gardening that was a little more artistic, that had a more permanent landscape feeling. He wanted a garden that would have a beautiful structure even when the plants were not in bloom. Rock gardening was the answer. He found that he could achieve the permanence he wanted with rock. "Or," he says, "if you're not using rock, you can use the many shrubs and evergreens that create a foundation so that as the perennials die down and go to sleep the garden still has a beautiful landscape effect. Also, a rock garden is part of the naturalistic landscape that I like."

Mineo isn't dogmatic about keeping his landscape universally in a "natural" style, however. As his garden has expanded (and it is constantly growing), he has found it convenient to lay out parts of it in straight lines, in a more formal fashion. The rock gardens have adapted well to that, too. Indeed, one of the things he values most about a rock garden is its adaptability.

His garden provides a number of different environments in which alpines and other rock plants grow. There are raised beds, troughs, and even pots of all shapes and sizes. A crevice garden in the form of a mountain, designed by a Czech gardener who specializes in building crevice gardens, has proved enormously successful for growing some of the most difficult little alpines in crevices. It has been so successful, in fact, that in 1995

Mineo developed what he calls a "concrete crevice bed" to create more crevices for plants.

To create the bed, he started with a few loads of broken concrete pieces from a sidewalk that was being removed from a neighbor's yard—though not a material of choice, the concrete chunks were free. Mineo piled them in a hot, dry spot. Then he added soil, planted the bed with plants that relish alkalinity and the lime that leaches out of the concrete, plants such as alpine pinks (*Dianthus* spp.) and saxifrages (*Saxifraga* spp.), and mulched with gravel. The concrete, he says, is hardly visible at all, and it still affords the protection from

> *The most favorable aspect of the local climate in southern Oregon is the winter drought.*

heat and excess moisture in winter (when there is the occasional long wet spell) that natural rock crevices would give. The concrete effectively moderates the available growing conditions, and the bed will require only minimum irrigation in summer.

The native soil in this part of Oregon is clay, so Mineo has built raised beds—some surrounded with wood, block, or brick—to improve drainage. The soil mix varies from bed to bed, depending on the plants growing there. Some beds contain pure sand and gravel, while others contain heavier, richer soil with some organic matter. He uses scree mixes of basically sand, grit, and some organic matter such as leaf mold or peat in varying proportions to create a very lean scree

or a richer scree. "We even add some sandy loam when we want it richer," he explains.

In the crevices, heavier soil is the rule. "For plants that require the same excellent drainage as a scree bed, if you've got a deep crevice, you want to fill that crevice with a much richer soil, not a scree soil at all," Mineo says. A light scree mix would eventually wash out of the crevice or sink. "We use a much heavier soil, even a clay loam, in a crevice to provide what little soil the plant will have." When customers ask if a particular plant can be grown in a scree, Mineo often surprises them by replying, "Yes, or you could grow it in clay in a crevice." In a wetter climate, that approach might not work as well, but in southern Oregon it works perfectly.

Irrigation is necessary during the dry summers, and most of the beds are mulched with gravel or chips. Because mold is not a problem in the dry climate, some of the beds that are home to dwarf shrubs and other nonalpine plants are mulched with bark, and the plants thrive.

Mineo grows a wide range of plants, everything from alpines to large perennials. "Being a nursery, we always try to acquire the newest and the best." The limiting factor is the heat of the local summers: a few of the more heat-sensitive ericaceous plants don't thrive at Siskiyou. Mediterranean plants that tolerate cold winters perform splendidly, however, and rare hardy geranium species flourish as well.

The most favorable aspect of the local climate, Mineo has found, is the winter drought. Most alpines will tolerate a summer hot spell so long as they are not exposed to the fatal combination of wet and cold in wintertime. Many high-mountain plants that lowland rock gardeners have traditionally cultivated in greenhouses are grown at Siskiyou without shelter.

What are Baldassare Mineo's favorite rock garden plants? He confesses to a special weakness for dwarf daphnes such as Daphne jasminea, and gentians of all sorts, both the dwarf alpine types and the taller perennial sorts. But even a cursory look through the Siskiyou Rare Plant Nursery catalog reveals how truly catholic this gardener's taste is—and how accommodating his garden is as well.

TROUGH GARDENING

Thinking big is the classic pattern among gardeners—the common impulse is to keep adding more and ever more area to garden. But the best of rock gardeners are more likely to think small. They find a special appeal in miniature plants, and they know that there are many advantages in growing these in miniature, self-contained landscapes. In short, they understand the advantages offered by trough gardens.

Many types of alpines adapt well to container cultivation, and indeed, gardeners have been growing alpine and rock plants in pots since the earliest days of rock gardening. Many sorts of containers are used for this purpose. Double-fired clay pots and strawberry jars are both popular, and they provide a very practical means of displaying compact plant specimens. But troughs offer that and something more. For in

This hypertufa trough is an ideal place to grow a wide selection of alpines. The pink-flowered erodium (Erodium × var.) is not hardy but continues to flower throughout the summer.

the broader expanse of a trough, a gardener can re-create a whole alpine landscape in miniature.

Actually, any large, weatherproof, and well-drained container will serve for this purpose. Troughs, however, are the classic solution, and the reason for

When creating a trough garden, choose only plants that are naturally dwarfed—otherwise, the garden will outgrow its home.

this has to do with the history of this type of miniature rock garden. Like so many other aspects of rock gardening, the idea of assembling different plants and small rocks in large planters to create miniature alpine landscapes originated in England in the early years of this century. At that time, hand-carved stone troughs were widely used for watering livestock. Stone containers of this sort must have seemed especially appropriate for the cultivation of rock plants and alpines; they were attractive and durable, and because they were abundant, they were also relatively inexpensive. Not surprisingly, they became the standard container among rock gardeners.

The modern American rock gardener does not have access to antique troughs of this sort, and yet trough gardening as a style of cultivation for rock garden plants is more popular now than ever before. That's because it offers a unique sort of flexibility, and the opportunity for gardeners to grow plants that would not otherwise survive in their locales. So, for example, southern gardeners can grow alpines that would not normally survive their sum-

mers by planting them in troughs that they move to the shelter of a shaded, well-ventilated cold frame. Northern gardeners can cultivate plants that would not normally overwinter in their regions by growing them in troughs that they move into shelter through the coldest months. Troughs are ideal for the cultivation of rare specimens that might be lost in the regular rock garden. And the owner of the smallest yard can still find space for several different kinds of alpine landscapes—by cultivating them in a row of troughs.

A trough garden will flourish in a wide range of planters, from a large bonsai tray to a window box. The most economical type of container, and one that has a rugged look well suited to rock garden plants, is the trough that the rock gardener himself makes from "hypertufa." This is a special type of concrete, which weathers to stonelike brownish gray (see pages 78–79 for step-by-step instructions for making this kind of trough).

When creating a trough garden, it is essential to choose only plants that are naturally dwarfed—otherwise, the garden will soon outgrow its home. Indeed, a trough garden is ideal for the cultivation of plants that are so delicate in scale that they have little visual impact in a normal rock garden. Another practical consideration to keep in mind when selecting plants for a trough garden is that all must be mutually compatible. That is, all the various species must thrive in similar conditions of light and exposure, and that prefer the same kind of soil. In general, this soil should be free-draining but also moisture retentive. A mix of equal parts leaf mold, sharp sand, and loam works well for most plants, though this will have to be emended with an extra part sand (or even two) for plants that require extra-good drainage and a light soil, such as *Aethionema* (Persian stone cress) or *Arenaria* (sandwort), or with an extra part or two of leaf mold for plants that prefer a humusy soil, such as gentians.

Set the trough in its ultimate home *before* planting it—it is much easier to move before it has been filled with soil and plants. Line the bottom with a sheet of fiberglass window screen to keep the potting soil mix from running out the drainage holes. Then fill the trough with soil mix; the traditional practice of covering the container's bottom with a "drainage" layer of gravel or broken clay pot shards has been found to be unnecessary. Form the soil into a topography that pleases you and add any stones you intend to include in the trough landscape. The rules for arranging stones in a trough are the same as those that apply to any other rock garden, except, of course, the stones in a trough must be small if they are to be in scale with the plants and the container.

Troughs need consistent watering, especially during the heat of summer, but should not be overwatered. The best rule is to let the soil schedule the irrigation: water whenever the soil is dry, but let it dry out between waterings. Fertilize sparingly, for too generous feeding encourages fast, soft growth that is prone to diseases and rot, and may provoke even dwarf species to outgrow their containers.

Because they lack the deep root-run of ordinary garden beds, troughs are especially vulnerable to summer heat, and in the South they should be

By selecting plants with thought to foliage as well as flower, an artificial trough can be an attractive feature all season long, filled with a variety of colors, shapes, and textures.

moved to an area of dappled shade through the hottest months. Troughs are also more vulnerable to cold. In areas where winters are mild (zones 8–9) the troughs may be overwintered in place, though burying them in a blanket of evergreen boughs during the coldest weeks will reduce frost damage. Where winters are moderate (zones 6–7), troughs should be set on the ground in a sheltered location, perhaps underneath evergreen shrubs, and tucked in with mulch around the trough and the same covering of evergreen boughs.

In really cold regions (zone 5 and north), troughs are best overwintered in a cold frame. In the absence of a cold frame, a trough may be overwintered successfully in the shelter of an unheated but enclosed sunporch. Be sure to ventilate the porch on sunny, mild days so that the temperature inside doesn't soar, since sudden spikes of heat are almost as harmful to the dormant trough plants as extremes of cold. Water as necessary, but keep in mind that dormant plants need less moisture than those in active growth, and that a combination of cold temperatures and water-logged soil is fatal to alpine and rock plants.

With a little care, a trough garden will also tolerate overwintering in an unheated garage. Wait until cold weather has caused the plants to go truly dormant before moving the trough into this kind of shelter. Water only very occasionally: the object should be to keep the soil just slightly moist so that the plants do not dehydrate. Take care not to wet the foliage —plants are especially prone to rot in the dark environment of the garage. Then return the trough to the outdoors as soon as temperatures moderate, so that the warming weather of early spring does not cause the trough plants to resume growth while they are still stored away in darkness.

MAKING A HYPERTUFA TROUGH

1) When Robert Bartolomei makes a hypertufa trough, he begins by making the form in which it is cast. For a rectangular trough, he creates the form from two cardboard boxes, one larger than the other. The larger box serves as the outside of the form; the smaller box, which is the form's interior, must be 2 inches smaller in both width and length.

Robert sets the larger box down on a flat, level space and then surrounds it with boards and concrete blocks to support its sides and prevent them from sagging or bowing outward when the form is filled with concrete. Then he paints the interior of this box with used motor oil so that the concrete will not attach itself to the cardboard.

2) The formula for hypertufa varies from gardener to gardener, and in fact there are almost as many recipes as there are trough gardeners. The basic ingredient is always Portland cement, but to this may be added all sorts of different ingredients such as sphagnum peat and vermiculite that are designed to lighten the trough while also giving it an earthy, stonelike look.

At NYBG, Robert Bartolomei uses a mix of equal parts Portland cement and horticultural perlite. To this he adds a handful of polypropylene fibers, a product that is designed to reinforce the concrete and which is available at most masonry supply stores. He also adds a polymer-based concrete hardener, another standard masonry supply, mixing this into the concrete at the rate recommended on the product label.

Then, after donning a pair of rubber gloves, Robert adds water slowly, turning and stirring the hypertufa mix with a mason's trowel as he does so. He adds enough water to thoroughly wet the mix, but he leaves it "stiff" rather than soupy.

3) When the hypertufa is mixed and ready, Robert trowels a 2-inch-thick layer into the bottom of the large cardboard box. Two-inch-long lengths of $\frac{1}{2}$-inch thick wooden dowels are pushed down through this layer of hypertufa; when they are removed later, they will leave drainage holes in the bottom of the finished trough.

4) Robert paints the exterior of the smaller box with motor oil and sets it down on top of the hypertufa inside the larger box. He centers the smaller box so that there is an even 2-inch space between it and the larger box all the way around.

5) Robert trowels moistened hypertufa mix into the space between the smaller and larger boxes, firming it in with the end of a small wooden board. As the hypertufa rises around the sides of the smaller box, Robert fills the box with gravel to keep its sides from collapsing inward.

6) When the side walls of the trough have been built up to the desired height, Robert stops adding hypertufa. He does not move or disturb the trough and form for 12 hours to let the hypertufa set. Then he removes the gravel from the inte-

rior box and tears off the cardboard from both the inside and outside of the trough. The trough is now ready for finishing, but is still in a fragile condition and so must be handled carefully.

7) The dowel plugs are slipped out of the bottom of the trough with a twisting motion, and the sides are wire-brushed to create a grained effect. The edges and corners are rounded off with a flat piece of iron. Any polypropylene fibers that stick out from the hypertufa are burned off with a propane torch.

8) After the finishing is completed, the trough must be cured and weathered. With a hose, Robert wets the trough well. Then he seals it in a plastic bag and sets it in a shady place. After leaving it there for a couple of weeks, Robert takes the trough out of the bag and leaves it out uncovered for a couple of months, to let the rain wash out any chemicals that may be harmful to plant growth. Once this weathering process is completed, the trough is ready for planting.

There are other methods of trough-making. A free-form container, for example, may be cast by troweling hypertufa over a form made of a lump damp sand. In this case, the outside of the sand form represents the interior of the finished trough, and the trough is cast upside-down. Be sure to make the top of the sand form flat so that the base of the trough will be flat, and push dowel plugs through the trough base while still wet to create drainage holes. Covering the form with a plastic drop-cloth before troweling on the hypertufa will help the trough set up better. Otherwise, the casting, finishing, and weathering process is the same.

Saxifraga aizoon.

3

CREATING
THE GARDEN

O ther kinds of gardens may begin with tilling and sowing, but the rock garden begins with rockwork: you have to build it before you can plant it. If a naturalistic garden is the goal and your yard is not endowed with outcrops and ledges, these features will have to be man-made, by collecting and installing the rocks. If the aim is to create a more architectural garden, dry stone walls, raised beds, or other structures must be constructed to form planting areas.

This book cannot cover all of the specialized skills required to build walls, and you may want to seek help from an experienced stone mason when you undertake such a project. But with a bit of effort and a few simple tools, any gardener can create a naturalistic rock garden, guided by Robert Bartolomei's step-by-step instructions.

SITE

When choosing a site for the rock garden, scrutinize the natural features of the property and try to work with them rather than struggling to transform them. A natural rock outcrop, for example, can become a focal point rather than an obstruction to be removed. Working with existing rock formations is obviously far easier than building them.

Topography. Even if no natural rock formations exist, select the topography that lends itself to creating them—ideally, an open area where the land is sloped gently, offering both optimal drainage and a tilted platform for the best display of plants. Although a flat site can be adapted with adequate drainage, planted walls and raised beds are more practical options for a property with an absolutely level grade.

Exposure. After examining the topography, consider exposure. An open location that receives sun for a good part of the day is best for many alpine and rock plants. But although sun is desirable, the sunniest of positions—a southern exposure—is not the best choice for many

Only nature could create such outcrops; this magnificent garden was formed by removing the overlying soil to expose the natural rock formations below.

of the classic alpines. In most North American climates, a garden facing south will be too hot for some rock plants in summer, and by exposing the plants to sun and drying winds in winter will decrease the chances for successful overwintering.

An eastern or northeastern exposure better suits the cultural needs of rock plants. East-facing gardens give the plants gentle morning sun; the stronger afternoon sun of west-facing gardens can cause fierce surges in temperature.

A garden with a northern exposure, because it is tilted away from the angle of the sun's rays in summer, is the best of all, especially if unobstructed by trees or buildings. A north-facing garden on a gentle slope offers a number of advantages for growing almost any kind of rock plant. When the sun rides low in the winter sky, its effect on the plants in such a garden is minimal; as a result, they remain in undisturbed dormancy, which reduces the chance of winterkill. Because a north slope is colder, snow tends to accumulate there and to remain longer, serving as an insulating blanket that protects plants underneath it from severe cold and drying winter winds.

Regional considerations. Finding the best site for your rock garden will be influenced to some degree by regional variations. Traditionally, rock gardeners have insisted on planting in sites open to full sun, but that is a legacy of the craft's European origins. In northern Europe, summers are cool and the sunlight less intense. This is also the case in northerly and coastal regions of the United States, areas such as New England and the Pacific Northwest. But as rock gardening has spread throughout the United States, gardeners in regions where the summers are hot have found that some light shade in the afternoon is beneficial. Actually, such shade may benefit alpines even in cooler regions, since even there the heat of summer afternoons can be oppressive. If you are planting your rock garden with saxatile and Mediterranean plants, however, you will find that they do best in sites with unobstructed sun.

Manipulating exposure. The selection of the site alone is not the only factor in determining exposure. Placement of boulders, walls, and

other garden features can be manipulated to enhance light or shadow, thus marking out a limited space into different microclimates and vastly increasing the possibilities for a range of plant types. A spot to the south of a large rock, for example, because it is exposed to the sun and sheltered from the cold north wind, will be warmer than the surrounding garden. Walls and rocky outcrops and ledges all cast shade, especially on the north side, where conditions will be somewhat cooler. In fact, each side of an outcrop or mound offers a planting area with a different exposure, as do the walls of a raised bed. In a small valley in the garden, the environment on a north slope differs dramatically from that on a south slope, and a slope facing east is not like a western slope. Even the larger plants such as dwarf conifers and shrubs cast shade and offer shelter.

Garden setting. The final consideration in choosing a site for a rock garden is what lies beyond. What will be the setting for the garden

Lower and more level areas around rocky features provide opportunities to develop alpine meadow plantings, as in the T. H. Everett Rock Garden. OPPOSITE: Careful rock placement can create a multitude of shady nooks, cool retreats for the plants' roots in the heat of a lowland summer.

picture? Even the most cleverly composed outcrop will look odd if isolated in the middle of the lawn or positioned next to a hedge or other formal structure. Likewise, if the view beyond the rock garden is of the neighbor's swimming pool or the toolshed, the rock garden will inevitably appear artificial by contrast. Generally, the most effective backdrop for a rock garden is a group of conifers or large shrubs set some distance away. The trees or shrubs provide a neutral green backdrop, and one that appears natural rather than man-made.

AN INTRODUCTION TO STONE

Among the most critical influences on the decision to build a particular type of rock garden is the type of stone available. If a site already abounds with stone, the rock gardener is both blessed and cursed: he or she will have no difficulty in amassing appropriate materials, but will have to use what nature has deposited. Purchasing stone likewise involves compromises, however: the gardener is limited by what the budget will allow and also to the sizes and types of stone offered by local suppliers.

Problems with small rocks. The novice rock gardener should beware of small rocks. These are tempting, because they are easier to lift, move, and rearrange than large stones. Yet, ironically, small rocks are best left to the experts. Assembling many small rocks into a natural-looking, convincing composition requires both talent and experience. The novice's piles of rocks often look like just that—piles that have been randomly scattered around the site and do not give the impression of natural geology that is the aim of good rock garden design.

A naturalistic garden of outcrops and ledges is a style of rock garden especially suited to a beginner, since it is easier to achieve a convincing and attractive planting in such a setting. And such an arrangement of rocks *is* easy to work with, if nature has provided it. Keep in mind, though, that counterfeiting such a setting, especially if it involves the importation of materials, can be a laborious process. The construction of the rock features in NYBG's Everett garden, for example, required the labor of a crew of four to five workers and horses over a period of several years. Obviously, the construction of a small home garden is not such an overwhelming undertaking. But still, it is not a project to be begun casually.

To strike a balance between expense and aesthetic challenge, Bartolomei suggests that the beginner consider an architectural rather than a naturalistic approach and that they assemble small rocks into an obviously artificial but attractive raised bed or dry wall designed for planting.

Placement. But whether the rocks are small or large, careful placement is crucial because the rocks form not only the visual framework of the rock garden but the structural framework as well. The rocks are not just a background; they are an integral part of the garden itself, and their visual effect depends on an illusion of geological accuracy. To appear natural, each rock must seem related to all the others. Poorly placed rocks cannot be disguised by a mass of lovely plants; they will

A dry stone wall such as this provides a perfect habitat for crevice plants. This kind of more structured arrangement is far easier to incorporate into a small or formally landscaped yard than naturalistic rockwork.

always arrest attention, distracting from all of the other garden features. No matter how beautiful the plants, the garden will always seem somehow "off," not quite right.

Rock selection criteria. When selecting stone, the basic rule is that all the rocks in the garden should be of the same geological type. It is most appropriate to use local stone, if possible, obtained from a local quarry if not on site. But even if the rocks come from a distant source, they should share a common origin.

Look at any of your rocks carefully and you may notice that it has strata, a sort of grain, almost like that of a piece of wood (this is not true of all stone). If your garden is to have a natural look, the strata of all the rocks should run in the same direction—even if you are building something artificial such as a stone wall, mismatching the stone's strata may give the structure an awkward appearance.

Doing your homework. For clues about matching and assembling rocks, spend some time studying natural rock outcrops in your area, and draw your inspiration from what nature has done so well. When designing the look of an outcrop or ledge, think about the rocks as aboveground projections of a single large mass. By matching up the strata in different rocks to follow the same direction, and by assembling rocks in ways that give the illusion that they are all part of a larger underground formation, you can make strong visual lines that unify the garden and alleviate the sense of busyness that so many small plants can otherwise project.

Well-constructed ledges provide ideal growing conditions and the most advantageous positions to view colorful rock plants such as these moss phloxes, dianthus pulsatilla, and basket-of-gold.

Rock shapes. The shapes of individual rocks dictate how they should be used. For outcrops, Bartolomei prefers rocks with irregular, jagged edges and unusual shapes. Weathered rocks collected on site give the appearance of an old, long-exposed rock formation. An outcrop fashioned of rounded and smooth rocks will not appear natural, but such rocks can work well in a berm, since worn rocks are typically part of a glacial deposit. Assemble the largest boulders in groups toward and at the base of the berm as if they rolled there. Place smaller boulders around them and just a little farther up the berm.

Unless you have a wealth of stone on site, you will find that large rocks are an expensive luxury to be used sparingly. Grouping large boulders together will give them more visual weight than will scattering them about the garden. Above all, never place rocks in a regular pattern.

Working with rocks. To anchor a large rock in place, bury the base up to its widest point. This makes it look as if the rock gets larger underground, implying that it is connected to other rocks in the garden below the soil surface. It is not necessary, Bartolomei feels, to bury rocks to two-thirds of their height as is sometimes recommended. Just be sure they look (and are) firmly anchored so that they do not shift if pushed.

When possible, try to work with rocks without cutting or breaking them. For making outcrops or ledges, find rocks that more or less mate along the edges, and match the layers or strata, if the stone has them, and the colors as well. When building dry walls and raised beds, find stones that fit together reasonably well. Choosing which rocks to place where is time consuming, but the rewards begin as the garden takes shape.

Stone-cutting skills and tips. If necessary, stones can be shaped somewhat to enable them to fit better. With a mallet and a mason's stone chisel you can split a single stone in two, knock off a corner, or remove

Even rounded boulders can be assembled into a convincing rock garden, if set into a berm or tumbled together at the foot of a waterfall as they have been here.

lumps and bumps to flatten a surface. But these sorts of alterations should be kept to a minimum. The chiseled edge never looks as natural as it did before cutting, the process slows down construction, and for those not skilled with mason's tools, one false move can be expensive. And always remember that shaping or splitting rocks requires appropriate safety precautions. Wear safety goggles, heavy gloves, and sturdy work boots to protect yourself from flying and falling pieces of stone. If your budget permits, work with a skilled stonemason on the trickier parts of the job.

Building a rock garden is a complex process, and even with the best of efforts, a first attempt may not be entirely satisfying. As with all three-dimensional design, the problems may emerge only when the project is finished. Rather than immediately renovating the completed structure, Bartolomei recommends letting the garden stand for a season while you assess the design to understand how it works for the plants and where its problems are. Any adjustments will then be based on real knowledge.

WHAT KIND OF ROCK IS BEST?

Gardeners who possess a garden site that is naturally supplied with stone have the good fortune to be able to skip this important decision. But those who must buy the rock to build the garden face a multitude of choices that will greatly influence the final look of the garden.

As noted earlier, locally acquired rocks generally give a garden the most natural look, automatically blending with the existing geology of your site. As a rule, stone gathered from nature looks less artificial than stone from a quarry. When buying quarried stone, however, the sizes of individual rocks can be specified; gathered stone must be taken as it comes.

The type of rock selected will influence not only the look of the finished garden but also the quality of plant growth. Softer types of stone such as sandstone and limestone, for example, are especially useful for gardens in dry climates, since such rocks typically absorb moisture and serve as an additional reservoir for the plants.

Tufa. The Cadillac of rocks, as far as plant growth is concerned, is tufa, a type of soft, porous limestone that comes from lime-rich springs. Tufa is gray in color and has an irregular, pitted surface into which plants can actually send roots. In fact, some plants will thrive planted directly into holes drilled into tufa. Moreover, tufa's neutral color makes an excellent setting for all plants. Unfortunately, tufa is hard to obtain and expensive when it is available.

Limestone. Other kinds of limestone also make excellent materials for rock gardening, however. Limestones tend to have lots of character—very visible striations that add visual interest in the garden. And though other kinds may not be as absorbent as tufa, limestones are in general porous and to some degree will serve as reservoirs of moisture. Mosses and lichens grow freely on limestone's porous surface, and because it is a soft stone and fractures relatively easily, limestone usually offers many crevices into which small plants can seed themselves. Limestone is usually whitish to gray in color.

Sandstone. Another soft rock, sandstone is more amorphous in shape and so is less distinctive than limestone, but it is still a good choice for a rock garden. Like limestone, sandstone absorbs moisture. Because it is soft, its surface weathers easily, often creating attractive textures and interesting patterns.

A soft, naturally porous limestone, tufa is the best rock for encouraging plant growth—but it is usually difficult to obtain and almost always expensive.

Granite and gneiss. Although they are very hard and nonab-sorbent, the rugged strength of granite and gneiss makes them out-standing for adding structure to the garden. A disadvantage of both of these rocks is that they are extremely difficult to shape with a chisel.

WORKING WITH GRAVEL

Gravel is, of course, an essential ingredient of a scree bed, and it is invaluable as a general mulch for the rock garden. For information on using gravel in scree beds, see "Scree Mixes" on page 97.

During his years at the Everett garden, Robert Bartolomei has found that laying down a gravel mulch is the single most effective way to reduce maintenance in the rock garden. An inch-thick layer of gravel prevents soil compaction and erosion by breaking the force of heavy rains. Mulch also keeps mud from splashing onto the foliage and

A natural rock mulch surrounds and effectively protects this wild Androsace *villosa.*

flowers of the small plants, thus helping to reduce the threat of rot. It inhibits most weed seeds from germinating by blocking light, but at the same time it provides a good seedbed for rock plants and helps these desirable specimens to self-sow. Finally, like other mulches, a gravel mulch helps keep the soil cool and moist below the surface.

Choosing gravel. Whatever gravel you use should harmonize in color and texture with the larger rocks in the garden. Crushed basalt, bluestone, sandstone, quartz, and pea gravel are all common choices, and all will provide the horticultural benefits of weed control and soil protection. Ideally, gravel should not only blend in with the surrounding rocks but should also be of a color that sets off the flowers in the garden. At the very least, avoid using a bright white gravel, which is blinding and visually distracting.

A gravel mulch can provide aesthetic benefits; here, it ties together visually the rock ledges of the T. H. Everett Rock Garden. FOLLOWING PAGE: The gravel overspreading the soil around this cultivated Symphyandra wanneri *offers protection from weeds and soil compaction, and prevents mud from splashing on the blossoms.*

You may be able to obtain a screened gravel that is a different size than the gravel normally used in paving roads and thus less expensive. If you use a screened and graded gravel for mulch, choose a large size (¾ inch). Larger stones interrupt the capillary action of the soil that draws water up from subsurface reserves, so that the surface is kept dry around plant crowns while the deeper soil stays moist.

Sources. When shopping for gravel, try to make a selection from locally mined sources, not only because it will probably be the most natural looking but also because it is the most likely to be available in the future. If you buy a gravel that is trucked in from a distant source, make sure that it is of a kind that has been used locally for some time and

that suppliers plan on continuing to stock it. If not, you may be forced to switch to a different kind of gravel, and your mulch will begin to look like a mineral hodgepodge rather than a natural deposit.

SOILS FOR THE ROCK GARDEN

Because the rock gardener's goal is to provide plants not just with growing space but with an environment, soil composition is of special concern. Unlike soils for almost any other type of gardening, most rock garden soils are man-made mixes instead of somewhat improved versions of what is found on the site.

The pains that experienced rock gardeners such as Robert Bartolomei take in preparing their soils may seem extreme, but when trouble strikes the rock garden, the underlying problem is often the soil. A fungal disease may have ultimately killed the favorite plant, but what set the stage for infection was soggy, poorly drained soil. Or, after thriving the first year, plants may gradually lose their vigor, as poorly balanced soil settles and compacts.

There is no magic recipe for rock garden soil, no single mix that will suit every plant, or suit even a single species in every climate or every garden situation. But developing a suitable mix for the needs of your garden need not be complicated.

Depth of soil mix. As a rule, the soil mix in any type of rock garden should be at least 1 foot deep. Remember as you mix the different elements—gravel, topsoil, compost, and so on—that interlocking relationships are at work in the soil. Like any plant, alpine and rock species require a continuous supply of moisture to the roots, and this comes from water moving through the pores between the soil particles; these pores also serve as drains through which excess water escapes. Roots need oxygen, too, and they need a way to vent the potentially toxic carbon dioxide they produce as a waste product—the pores are essential here as well.

Porosity. It is hard to overestimate the importance of maintaining good soil porosity—what is usually referred to as aeration—for keeping rock plants healthy and vigorous. No garden plant benefits from a compacted, airless soil, but alpines and rock plants demand an even looser mix. A porous, well-aerated soil provides the kind of fast drainage that rock plants require, and a well-aerated soil encourages deep and vigorous root systems, which the plants need to absorb moisture and nutrients.

The degree of aeration required in the rock garden varies with climate; a wet climate demands an extra-loose, rapid-draining, and hyperaerated soil. For all climates, drainage and aeration should be planned with the wettest part of the growing season in mind. Plants may require watering during spells of dry weather, but their long-term survival will be assured.

Along with the manipulation of exposures, as described earlier, growing conditions can be adjusted to suit individual niches by varying the soil mix. A lean scree soil produces a drier environment, whereas a soil containing more humus yields moister conditions. For a particularly diverse garden, Bartolomei recommends using leaner, faster-draining soils in the higher parts of the garden and moisture-retaining soil mixes lower on the slope. The different soil mixes exaggerate what are natural tendencies—lower-lying areas naturally collect moisture—and make a wider range of plant life possible within a very small garden area.

Standard rock garden soil mix. The traditional recommendation calls for a 1:1:1 ratio of gravel and/or coarse sand, topsoil, and compost, with the addition of ground dolomitic limestone as necessary to raise the pH to about 6.5. This is still an excellent soil mix for most rock garden plants and will work well for an alpine meadow planting. Depending on the region, however, the standard mix may need adaptation. For example, superphosphate should be added in regions where the soil tends to be deficient in phosphorus; and in high-rainfall areas of the coastal Northeast or the South, an extra part of the gravel and coarse sand should be added to boost aeration. If the topsoil is heavy—that is, if it is rich in clay and thus sticky and impermeable—the quantity of topsoil in the mix should be reduced. The only true determination of the "best" soil mix is whether the garden thrives; if you know successful rock gardeners in your area, ask them how they mix their soil.

Scree mixes. The scree soil mix is far more versatile today than it was in the past. No longer confined solely to use in scree beds, scree mixes are used by rock gardeners in a variety of situations. Indeed, some gardens are created using nothing else. The popularity of scree mixes is easy to understand: they are simple and inexpensive to produce and so are easy to custom-blend for different applications. As a group, scree mixes lend themselves to the cultivation of a wide range of choice alpines and other rock plants. They are especially useful where the climate is moist and summers are humid.

A basic scree mix contains four parts gravel of mixed sizes blended and one part loam and compost combined, but the basic mix will need adjustment to suit local conditions. In wetter climates and moister parts of the garden, the proportion of loam and compost in the mix should be leaner. Even if the garden will experience only certain periods

New York City's hot, humid summers are a trial for most alpines and rock plants— but the scree bed in the T. H. Everett Rock Garden serves as refuge to species that might otherwise succumb to rot.

of extra moisture, you may want to consider thinning the scree mix; a leaner mix will protect plants from rotting during summers of heavy and continuous rainfall, and through warm wet spells in winter. The balance of the mix may also be affected by the quality of the ingredients you find available locally. If the gravel you use is moisture absorbent, reduce the amount of soil and humus you mix with it to prevent the scree mix from becoming water retentive. On the other hand, if your gravel is made of hard stone, such as quartz or granite, like pea gravel, you will need to incorporate a higher proportion of moisture-retentive material into your scree mix.

Bartolomei emphasizes that a scree mix must include a variety of particle sizes, since uniform particles can lead to a break in the capillarity that draws water through the soil and furnishes moisture to plant roots. If all the gravel is coarse, for example, the air spaces will be too large, so the mix will always be bone-dry and plants will be unable to send roots down through it. The water must drain through quickly, yet moisture must be able to "wick" back up through smaller air spaces in the mix to supply the roots of the plants.

Ironically, although most uniniti-ated gardeners think of a meadow as a field of weeds and wildflowers, an alpine meadow requires consid-erable advance preparation.

Achieving a good blend may take extra planning if the only gravels available are screened and graded gravels, which have been sifted mechanically to ensure that all the particles in a particular batch are of a uniform size. If you must buy such gravels, purchase small lots of several sizes and then mix them, adding in some coarse sand as well. Get coarse builder's sand from a mason's supply company, and make sure what you buy is the "sharp," pebbly kind used in making concrete; never use fine beach or river sand in the rock garden.

After blending the different ingredients of your scree mix, test the result by heaping it up and pouring water over it, enough water to wet the heap thoroughly. Check the mix a few days later: the surface should be dry, but a few inches in, the mix should still feel slightly moist and cool.

When you lay a scree mix over existing soil, some of the mix must be incorporated into the existing soil before the remainder is spread on top. Discrete layers of soil would establish a boundary that would block the downward and upward movement of moisture. During wet weather, water draining through the scree mix would likely collect in a puddle on top of the soil below, causing roots to rot; during dry weather, moisture would not wick up from the soil and back into the scree. Not only would these extremes in moisture harm plants in the short term but such a barrier would also discourage them from establishing deep, drought-resistant root systems.

At NYBG, Bartolomei constructs a scree bed in several steps. First, he excavates the existing soil to a depth of at least 1 foot. Next, he loosens the subsoil and chops it into clods (not small bits). Then he spreads a couple of inches of the scree mix on top of the loosened subsoil and forks the two together (avoiding mixing them so well that a third stratum is created). Finally, he fills the bed with scree mix.

Sand beds. Making a sand bed is a similar process, and the same caveats apply. Again, excavate 12 inches of topsoil from the bed's site and loosen the subsoil as described above. Incorporate some sand lightly into the loosened subsoil. Then simply spread the sand on top, to a depth of 1 foot.

To keep the surface of the sand bed from forming a crust, incorporate some gravel into the top part of the sand layer before planting, and apply a gravel mulch after planting.

Alpine meadows. The soil in natural alpine meadows is fine textured, containing substantial amounts of minerals and organic matter. This is simulated in the rock garden with standard rock garden soil.

Ironically, although most uninitiated gardeners think of a "meadow" as a catchall term for a field of weeds and wildflowers, an alpine meadow requires considerable preparation. First, remove the sod if the area is currently a lawn. and eliminate any weeds. Till the soil and remove stones and roots to create a fine texture. If the soil is sandy or clayey, work in organic matter to improve the texture. If the soil is fertile and loamy, make it leaner by working in coarse sand or gravel. The soil should be tested for pH; you can either use a home testing kit (available at most garden centers) or send a sample to a state soil-testing laboratory (consult your local Cooperative Extension office for names of labs in your area). If the soil is acid, add enough lime to raise the pH close to neutral. The area can be mulched with gravel, which will not be visible when the plants knit together.

Once established after two to three years, however, an alpine meadow becomes a low-maintenance garden. Pull any weeds that sprout among the plants, and remove aggressive specimens that threaten to crowd out their neighbors.

PATHS AND ACCESS

The porous soil that has been so laboriously mixed and installed in the rock garden is easily compacted by foot traffic, so planning for access to plants is part of every good garden design. All the necessary chores of maintenance—weeding, watering, and planting—must be carried out without stepping onto a bed or dancing through it with the techniques of an acrobat.

Paths are a necessity in the rock garden, protecting the soil against compaction from foot traffic; every area of the garden should be accessible for weeding and other maintenance chores, without a need to step into the beds. OPPOSITE: A well-planned path also provides a convenient setting for the display of small specimens that might be lost if planted amid other, bolder plants.

In short, there should be a path or steppingstone wherever anyone needs or wants to step. Since many rock plants require closeup viewing to be appreciated, paths are also essential to the aesthetics of the rock garden: they should be laid out so as to allow the gardener and visitors alike to stroll through the garden and get to know the plants. If the paths are designed correctly, all the plants (no matter how small) will be visible from them.

Access. Providing access does not mean turning the garden into a network of trafficways. Two to 3 feet is a comfortable width for a main path, but the smaller, maintenance paths can be as narrow as 1 foot. Small plants should be set near a path, near enough to be viewed easily but not so near that an accidental misstep will crush them.

Choosing path materials. Paths will blend best into the garden design if they are surfaced with materials in keeping with the garden. Gravel or paving stones of a rock similar to the rocks used in constructing planting areas are good possibilities. Paths through woodland and other shady rock gardens may be surfaced with pine needles, wood chips, or shredded bark. For a path across a bog area, thick stepping-stones or rounds cut from a log will keep feet dry.

A trick that will help integrate almost any path into the garden is to plant low carpet-forming plants along the verges that will grow in to embrace it. Creeping thyme (*Thymus praecox* ssp. *arcticus*) and Corsican mint (*Mentha requienii*), for example, which tolerate foot traffic well and thrive in full sun, do a fine job of softening the edges of a flagstone path. And the scent they release when trod upon enhances the garden stroll.

A well-conceived and well-built path can become a decorative element in the garden, offering a domesticated contrast to the naturalistic rock work around it. OPPOSITE: An ingenious gardener has turned a flight of steps into a novel kind of rock garden, planting pockets among the stones with rosy-flowered Dianthus chinensis, *white-blossomed candytuft* (Iberis sempervirens), *and red sunroses* (Helianthemum nummularium).

This corkscrew hazel (Corylus avellana 'Contorta') contributes a strong form to the T. H. Everett Rock Garden, especially when winter robs the shrub of its foliage.

PLANTS FOR THE ROCK GARDEN

Having assembled all the "hardscape" of the rock garden—all the inanimate elements—the time has come to select the plants.

This book has already touched on a number of criteria by which to select plants for the rock garden. The plants should be of a modest scale so that they do not visually overwhelm the true alpines, and any nonalpines should not be aggressive spreaders that will crowd out the less robust rock plants. Perhaps the most useful way to approach the selection process, though, is to think in terms of the role that each type of plant will fulfill in the garden. Prospective choices can then be scrutinized to see if they can serve the purposes to which they will be applied.

The white froth of this Deutzia gracilis *'Nikko' pouring down over the gravel mulch illustrates one way in which floral shrubs can contribute form, texture, mass, and, of course, color to the rock garden.*

Structural plants. Rocks fix the basic structure of the rock garden, but larger plants can also play an important part in reinforcing and amplifying the "geology." All the plants contribute to some extent, but the decisive landscaping role is played by dwarf evergreens and small shrubs. Dwarf conifers provide height, form, texture, and mass; shrubs may also provide flowers, but their greatest value is as structural elements. The shrub's bloom, though often spectacular, is fleeting, but the impact of its form lasts all year.

For the structural plants to work well together, each must relate to the others. The plantsman's inclination may be to dot the conifers and shrubs about the garden so that each may be appreciated individually, but it is far more effective to plant them in groups at the back of the rock garden, off to the side, and even a few at a time in the foreground to create a sense of depth. Bartolomei finds that grouping together one species or variety and repeating this assemblage throughout the garden helps to unify separate areas into a total overall composition and visually anchors the garden into its surroundings.

When a berm, outcrop, or large ledge is part of the rock garden, special care needs to be taken to enhance rather than detract from the impact of such a feature. The effect of height of an outcrop or ledge will be diminished by a narrowly upright or conical conifer, such as a dwarf Alberta spruce (*Picea glauca* 'Conica'), at the top, which will make it appear squat. Instead, plant uprights in the foreground, with the rock garden behind. A better choice for the top of the feature is a fine-textured conifer with a mounded form, such as *Juniperus procumbens* 'Nana'. A delicate-looking plant of this sort adds more of an impression of height, mass, and depth to the garden. Around the

Dwarf conifers such as these can be most effective when grouped together mainly in the background, supplying the garden with a sense of depth and structure.

bottom of a slope or the base of the garden, broad-leaved evergreen or deciduous shrubs can replace conifers.

Purchasing considerations. Dwarf conifers are undeniably appealing in the rock garden, but it is best to limit their number, since they increase in height and spread—albeit slowly—and too generous a planting of them will eventually swallow up the garden. Before purchasing any dwarf conifers, make sure that those particular cultivars are truly dwarf. Some conifers that are sold as dwarf are not true dwarfs, as with many of the cultivars of *Chamaecyparis,* such as *C. obtusa* 'Crippsii', the golden Hinoki cypress, and *C. pisifera* 'Plumosa', a form of the Sawara cypress. These may be small when they arrive in your garden, but in as little as five years they can ruin the garden's sense of scale. Unless the plants will tolerate severe pruning, they will have to be removed.

One way to judge the growth rate of a conifer is to examine the new growth. Look at the candles of pines and the shoot tips of spruces and other dwarf conifers to see how much a young tree has grown during the current season. A dwarf with only ½ inch of new growth promises to be an excellent candidate for the rock garden. A conifer with 6 inches or more of new growth is much too fast-growing.

If after some years your conifers begin to outgrow the garden, you may be able to cut them back. You can control some of the low-growing junipers and pines with annual pruning. But some conifers, such as spruces, cannot be pruned back hard without uncovering bare branches that will never grow new needles.

Some rock gardeners become so enamored of dwarf conifers that they rely solely on them as structural plants in the garden. But there are a host of other small shrubs that suit rock gardens equally well. A dwarf lilac, *Syringa* 'Palibin' (syn. *S. palibiniana*), will grace the garden with fragrant lavender flowers on a 3- to 4-foot shrub in spring. *Deutzia gracilis* 'Nikko' forms a low ground cover, the branches rooting where they touch the ground. White bell-shaped flowers cover the shrub in spring and the foliage turns red in the fall. Dwarf willows, shrubby potentillas, and dwarf rhododendrons are also available, as

This pine has been dwarfed and sculpted by the severe mountain weather of the Sierra Nevadas. Genetically dwarfed conifers can be used to similar effect in the rock garden.

Every spring, the dwarf lilac Syringa *'Pali-bin' fills its corner of the T. H. Everett Rock garden with color and perfume.*

well as daphnes and cotoneasters suitable for the rock garden. Heaths and heathers too can function as structural shrubs in a rock garden, especially where the soil is sandy and acidic. Once conifers and shrubs are in place, it is time to consider the smaller plants.

Ground covers and herbaceous plants. How you arrange your collection of alpines and herbaceous (that is, nonwoody) plants within the rock garden will be dictated somewhat by personal taste but even more by the needs of the plants. Learn the cultural needs of every plant before bringing it home, and take care to provide the right exposure, soil, and level of moisture for each. Also think of your garden as a natural piece of geology, and try to follow nature's rules for plant arrangement. This will keep you from creating an unbalanced composition that is subtly (or perhaps not so subtly) jarring to the eye.

For example, if the focal point of the garden is a large and impressive rock, be aware that the erosive forces that would expose such a rock in nature would wash most of the soil off its top. It is not the place to install a relatively large or lush plant. The largest plants belong at the base of the rock, or at the lower levels of the rock garden where soil accumulates in a natural situation, and even in an artificial one. Among the many plants that work well for this purpose in a large rock garden are such familiar perennials as *Bergenia* and dwarf bearded irises. In a smaller garden, *Heuchera, Alchemilla,* and basket-of-gold (*Aurinia saxatilis*) work well. And remember that unless you are on your hands and knees, you will be looking at ground level from above.

Around the primary plants at ground level consider massing a ground cover of mat-forming plants. In the NYBG alpine meadow, Bartolomei has scattered small groups of spring-flowering bulbs to furnish color early in the season and included a summer-flowering ground cover (one of the many hardy thymes) to extend the display.

Obviously, the smallest and choicest plants should be set where they can be seen best, farther up rocky slopes. Even higher up, where the soils would be thinner and drier in nature, and the plants more exposed to the elements, ground-hugging and drought-tolerant mat-forming plants are the natural choice.

THE PASQUE FLOWER (ANEMONE PULSATILLA)

4

PLANTING
AND MAINTAINING
THE GARDEN

T he goal of most gardening is to establish plants that flourish year after year, but rock gardeners must accept that the longevity of their plants is, at least to some extent, out of their hands. Poor care will, of course, quickly kill most rock plants, but skillful cultivation does not necessarily ensure a long life span. The longevity of rock plants depends on several factors: the climate from year to year, the growing conditions in the garden itself, and the skill of the gardener. But the ultimate determinant is the species of plant.

Rock plants may live for many years a specimen of *Globularia cordifolia*, the heartleaf globe daisy, in the T. H. Everett Rock Garden has been there for 40 years. And some of the phloxes there are 20-year veterans. But as Robert Bartolomei is quick to admit, many of his other plantings have disappeared after a couple of seasons, no matter how carefully he nurtured them.

Nevertheless, many alpine plants from high elevations are unlikely to live more than two to three years in a low-altitude garden. Not even the horticulturists know the exact reasons for the shortened life spans, but it may be that the longer growing season at lower altitudes exhausts the plants—they literally grow and bloom themselves to death. Or the garden climate may simply be too stressful for plants adapted to life on the peaks. Other types of rock plants sometimes also succumb to the rigors of an unusually tough growing season—a summer of higher than average temperatures, or too much rain. Sometimes, too, like other kinds of garden plants, plants will fall victim to diseases or pests.

When plants such as the alpine poppy (*Papaver alpinum*), which is adapted to life in disturbed or unstable soils, set seed freely, they continually replace themselves with volunteer seedlings. But no matter the type of rock garden you have or the amount of care the plants receive, some replanting must be done every year.

This is not wholly a disadvantage. A need to keep replacing losses gives you a chance to keep trying new plants, so that the garden is constantly changing and never becomes boring. Other gardeners must often hunt for a spot to wedge in a new plant; in the rock garden, there is always room for that new plant you have been just dying to try.

PLANTING

One of the best sources of plants for the rock garden is mail-order nurseries, several of which are listed in Appendix A. Their catalogs offer an enormous selection of species and cultivars, and a good nursery will deliver plants in vigorous health, ready to grow. To give the plants the best start, try to be at home when they arrive so that they do not spend a day on the front steps baking in a hot sun or freezing in a chilly wind. Get the plants into a cool (but not cold) storage area as soon as possible. Resist the urge to pop them right into the garden. New arrivals need time to recover from the rigors of shipping before they are planted out.

Inspecting new plants. Mail-order plants are often shipped bare-root—that is, they have been dug from the nursery's growing area, stored without soil around the roots in a cold cellar, and then packed into mailing cartons with the roots swathed in a damp medium such as excelsior. With any bare-root plants, it is important to inspect the roots as soon as the shipment arrives. Unpack the plants immediately, remove the packing material from around the roots, and look them over. Both roots and crowns should be firm and be free of mold or shriveling. Clip off any broken or damaged roots at this time. Then pot up the plants as described below.

Plants may also be shipped with soil packed around the roots. Prepare such plants for potting by loosening the soil ball, which is likely to have been compressed during shipping. Use a pencil or chopstick to gently break up the packed soil and to remove any moss that may have grown on it.

Potting in containers. Whether the plants arrived bare-root or with soil, they should next be potted up into containers of a moist, porous, lightweight potting mix. Afterward they should be set in a cool but sheltered spot such as a shady cold frame or under the eaves against the north wall of the house. Allow the plants to convalesce there for 7 to 10 days, or even longer if they arrived from the nursery early and the weather is too cold and wet for transplanting.

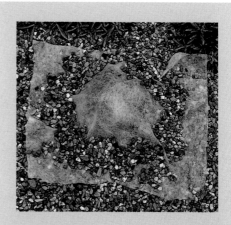

If you have no suitable area to hold the plants or must for some other reason set them out in the garden as soon as you receive them, plant them (this procedure is illustrated on pages 118–119) and then

A piece of floating row cover has been used here to protect a newly planted alpine from excessive sun. It should be removed one week later. FOLLOWING PAGE: Though spring is the season of greatest bloom, autumn brings not only its warm palette of colors to the T. H. Everett Rock Garden but ideal weather for planting as well.

cover them with a piece of a floating row cover. These covers, sometimes called garden blankets, are made of lightweight spunbonded polyester and sit lightly atop plants without weighing them down; they allow light and air to reach the plants but shield them from the

wind and keep them somewhat warmer. This protection will help the new plants adjust to life in the garden with far less trauma.

Watering new plants. Keep new plants watered until they become established. Even drought-tolerant plants need a regular supply of moisture until they have developed a good root system and settled into the garden, and neglecting irrigation during dry weather is likely to prove a death sentence. If the garden is brand-new, then you may water with a sprinkler —all the plants will require irrigation. But if the garden is an established one, then spot-water only, for although the new plantings may need the extra water, applying it too frequently to established plants may cause them to rot.

Although most gardeners think of spring as planting season, in many regions autumn is an excellent time to set out new rock plants.

In early to mid-spring, when the temperature is cool and rainfall tends to be more abundant, new plants will establish themselves quickly and watering can be discontinued after a month. But if the plants were shipped in late spring, watering will probably have to continue for a longer period to carry them through warmer weather.

Avoid planting during hot summer weather if at all possible. If you must, plant in the early morning. Give plants plenty of water and some shade, too, as they settle into the garden.

Timing. Although most gardeners think of spring as planting season, in many regions autumn is an excellent time to set out new rock plants. The mild fall weather allows plants to make good root growth with a minimum of stress. Be sure, however, to plant at least 6 to 8 weeks before the first fall frost date, so that plants have time to establish their root systems before they go dormant.

Planting procedure. When planting several plants in close proximity, plant them one at a time. Bartolomei's procedure is simple: Set aside the gravel mulch and dig the planting hole just a little larger than the size of the root ball. Position the crown of the plant so that the leaves will just rest on top of the mulch when it is replaced. When the plant is in the ground, water well. Then push the gravel mulch back in

1) *The gravel mulch is pushed well aside so* soil does not get mixed into it.
2) *To ease the new plant out of its container,* spread the fingers of one hand over the soil, up-end the pot, and tap it smartly on the bottom with the trowel. Then grasp the plant gently by its crown and ease it out of the pot.

3) *Any soil that has formed a crust around* the crown of the plant is removed and the root ball is loosened to ensure contact between the roots and soil in the bed.
4) *A chopstick is used to determined where the* crown of the plant needs to be positioned. It should be just at soil level.

place around the crown of the plant, and go on to the next plant. You may be tempted to clear the entire area of mulch and set all the plants at once. But planting en masse could result in planting too deeply. Without the mulch in place, Bartolomei explains, it is difficult to judge exactly how high the crown of the plant should be. Planting too deeply means too much water may collect in the depression around the roots

5) *The plant is held* in position while filling the planting hole with soil. Avoid leaving any air pockets, which would allow the plant to sink in later.

6) *The plant is patted* into place gently but firmly. This will help ensure that the roots will grow into the soil in the bed and not be confined to the planting hole.

7) *The mulching gravel* is pushed back into position and the foliage of the plant is held aside to bring the gravel right up under the crown.

8) *After a thorough watering* the plant is settled in its site and should begin to show signs of new growth in a couple of weeks.

and crown, which can cause rot. Planting too high can cause some roots to be exposed, which will rob the plant of moisture and nutrients. So take the extra time to plant individually. Learning to plant into mulch takes some practice and a sharp eye, but once you master the technique, your newly planted gems will give the impression that they have been in place for years.

FERTILIZING AND WATERING

Just because a lean, fast-draining soil mix is best for most rock plants, it does not follow that the plants do not need nutrients. On the contrary, fertilization (of the right sort) is particularly important to rock plants because the growing medium itself, especially in a scree or sand bed, holds so little nutrition.

Feeding. Instituting a rigid feeding schedule is nearly impossible. The appearance of the plants determines whether they need fertilizer, and overfeeding is as bad as underfeeding. If plants fail to perform well, particularly just after blooming, they probably need fertilizer.

When you do fertilize, avoid formulations high in nitrogen. A fertilizer made for tomatoes, or another product high in phosphorus and potassium but low in nitrogen, is best for rock plants. Best of all are the timed-release fertilizers, granulated products that feed plants gradually over a period of 3 months. But even with these, exercise care, reducing by a half the dosage of fertilizer recommended on the product label.

When applying granulated fertilizers, sprinkle them around each plant instead of broadcasting the granules over the entire bed. That way the nutrients are concentrated where they are easily accessible to the rock plants; broadcasting the fertilizer spreads the nutrients into areas where they benefit only weeds.

Watering. Adequate and regular moisture is also essential. In regions where rainfall is regular and abundant, irrigation may not be necessary at all, especially if the appropriate soil mix has been used. But in arid climates or during periods of drought, supplemental irrigation will be needed. Fast-draining screes and sand beds are likely to need more human intervention than alpine meadows and shady areas.

When you do water, be conservative, since overwatering on a regular basis can cause rot. Instead of setting up a sprinkler, hand-water only those plants in need. Be especially prudent during hot, muggy weather, when mildew and fungal diseases pose the greatest threat— and when the temptation to water abundantly is at its peak. Water adequately but sparingly, ideally, on a day when there is a breeze or at least some air movement. Never water at night, as water standing on leaves for hours increases their vulnerability to fungal infection. When watering late in the day, be sure that enough hours of sunlight remain to dry the foliage before sunset.

WEEDING AND MULCHING

Weeds require special attention in the rock garden, for invaders that would not be much of a problem in the perennial border can wreak havoc among the less aggressive alpines. Small rock plants in particular are easily overwhelmed by weeds. Crabgrass, if unopposed, will quickly engulf a rock garden, and oxalis spreads rapidly through the loose, gritty soil there, too. A lawn that runs right up to the perimeter of the rock garden poses an exceptionally serious threat. Once the grass has rooted up into the rocks' crevices or into a planted wall, it is practically impossible to remove. And a lawn dotted with clover is double trouble, for clover also spreads enthusiastically through the rock garden.

Hand-pulling vs. hoeing. Weeding a rock garden properly is a meticulous business. Hand-pulling, although slow, is the safest technique for keeping a rock garden weed-free. Hoeing is faster, but it is liable to decapitate small plants and is impractical in areas covered with mat plants. Weeding needs to be scrupulously thorough, so that the offenders are eradicated roots and all. Attacking the weeds while they are still young and shallow rooted, at the very least before they set seed, will save effort in the long run. Take the time to pick through the rock plants' crowns and remove any small weeds that may be coming up under the foliage. Once the weed is well rooted in, it may be impossible to remove it without disturbing its rock plant neighbor.

The easiest way to keep the rock garden weed-free is to stop the invasion before it starts.

Herbicide. The easiest way to keep the rock garden weed-free is to stop the invasion before it starts. An application of preemergent herbicide in early spring provides an effective deterrent by suppressing the germination of weed seeds—unfortunately, it will also prevent reseeding plants such as poppies from replacing themselves, and the long-term effect of these chemicals on the growth of established rock plants is largely unresearched. When setting new acquisitions into the garden, discard any excess soil in the shipping package and retain only the soil around the root ball; soil in nursery containers often harbors weed seeds.

Mulch. Mulch acts as a great weed suppressant. Keep a good blanket of gravel in place at all times, and don't let it become mixed with the soil below it. Try not to leave any openings in this protective barrier: when he must replace an old plant, Bartolomei fills in the hole with gravel mulch after digging out the root ball until he can replant.

Organic mulches are not suitable for most rock gardens. They shift more readily than a gravel mulch, and they soon accumulate in low-lying areas of the garden, where they smother anything planted there. Besides, they hold too much moisture around the base of rock plants.

One area where organic mulches are, however, appropriate is a woodland planting. The plants adapted to that environment respond well to a higher level of soil moisture and benefit from the humus such mulches provide as they decompose. Even here, though, you must choose the mulch with care. Wood chips, although cheap and abundant, do not stay in place; coarse compost or shredded leaves are easier to keep in place and provide the most natural appearance.

Defeating invaders. Sometimes plants invited into the garden can cause problems. Keep an eye on any plants that reseed or send out invasive runners, and make a point of promptly removing any unwanted seed heads or seedlings. Bugleweed (*Ajuga reptans*), a tempting quick cover choice for a novice rock gardener, may cause years of regret. In particular, make sure that the self-sowers don't sow themselves into the crowns of other plants.

In the end, the best tactic for weed prevention is to watch the garden's progress day by day. A problem caught early is a crisis avoided later on.

DEADHEADING AND PRUNING

Whether or not you deadhead in the rock garden involves a decision. Which is more important: the vigor of the plant or the harvest of seed?

Deadheading. Removing flowers as they fade—deadheading—prevents plants from setting seed. Essential for the survival of plants in nature, seed production can deplete the energy and slow the growth of the individual plant. If you don't need or want the seed, then deadhead. But given the transient quality of many rock plants, you may want to let the plants set seed so that they will replace themselves. In addition, self-sowers play a role in giving the rock garden the unstudied look that rock gardeners value, spontaneously filling out meadows and

Deadheading should be a regular part of maintenance, but the gardener may wish to forgo it if the seedheads are a large part of the plant's appeal, as in the case of the Pulsatilla vulgaris.

1) Using a sharp cutting tool such as scissors, cut back the invader to uncover the plant.

2) Depending on the vigor of the invader, cut back away from the plant to allow a season's growing space.

colonizing crevices in rocks and cracks in walls. Of course, such plants can become pests if they self-sow too enthusiastically, and when that is so, deadheading becomes a necessary form of control.

In the case of some favorite plants, however, you may not be willing to leave the job of sowing seed up to nature. You may want to harvest the seed and start seedlings yourself—or you may want to trade the seeds with another gardener to obtain seed of some other plant you covet. But even if you do decide to harvest seed, it is wise to conserve the plant's resources by deadheading most of the flowers. Leave several blossoms to set seed, but remove the rest.

The deadheading method depends on the type of plant. Rosette-forming plants, which tend to bear clusters of flowers atop upright stems and whose flowers tend to open all at once, can be deadheaded with a single cut at the base of the flower stem. With plants that send up branching flower stems on which the blossoms open over a period of time, cut back below each flower as it fades to the next set of leaves. The aim is to avoid snipping off just the flower head and leaving a bare stem.

*3) **Carefully pick out** any stems of the invader that may have rooted into the crown of the plant.*

*4) **Cut back** the mat-forming plant to reveal any rock that may have been covered.*

Pruning. A more severe application of the shears may be required from time to time, especially for the more vigorous mat-forming plants. These need periodic pruning to keep them in bounds. After flowering, simply trim back the edges of the mat with a sharp knife or shears.

Some mat-forming plants may also tend to die out at the center as they age. To rejuvenate such plants, clean out the old, dead central growth and top-dress the empty area with gravel mulch. Fertilize the plant, and the central portion should fill in again.

If you have chosen shrubs and conifers wisely, they should need very little pruning to keep them in scale. When conifers and shrubs are young, however, some pruning is necessary to shape them and to direct future growth. The bird's-nest spruces (*Picea abies* 'Nidiformis') in the T. H. Everett Rock Garden, for instance, are pruned after the first flush of spring growth. For their first few years, the tips of the upper tiers of branches are cut back to promote the outward growth·of the lower tiers; in this way, the shrub is encouraged to adopt a shapely, ground-hugging form. The dwarf chamaecyparises also receive an occasional

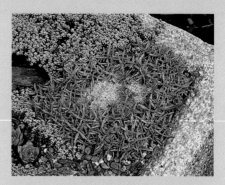

1) A cushion-forming plant has become thin in the center. Carefully cut out any dead stems and dress with dry sharp sand or mulching gravel to cover any bare stems.

2) The stems covered with the topdressing may send out roots and new stems, which after a time will fill in the gap.

light shearing. This gives them a pleasing shape, and if done only occasionally does not result in an artificial, formal profile.

Many dwarf conifers are genetically unstable, and a branch can revert to the larger, more vigorous normal form of the species. The first sign of this is the emergence of a fast-growing branch with the foliar characteristics of the parent. If neglected, this reversion will spoil the shape of the bush, and it is important to remove it promptly by cutting back to a spot a little bit below where the reversion begins.

WINTER CARE

To prepare the rock garden for winter, keep it free of fallen autumn leaves. If these pile up on top of rock garden plants, the plants quickly yellow and rot. The best tool for leaf removal is a small electric blower; a rake is likely to damage the plants unless handled very carefully.

Dianthus and other mounded and cushion plants also benefit from some special attention in fall to prevent crown rot in winter. Work a handful of coarse dry sand into the center of each plant. The extra sand speeds drainage of any water standing in the crown. This technique works especially well for plants that can root from the stems.

Once cold weather has set in, it is a good idea to cover the garden with evergreen boughs; this blanket serves the same function that snow cover does in the high mountains, shielding plants from drying winter winds and shading the soil to keep the ground frozen and so prevent frost heaving. The insulation may also keep plants from breaking dormancy too early—a serious threat to alpines, which are quick to start growth in the spring and may be fooled by a temporary winter thaw. Any growth that occurs then will almost certainly be killed when the cold weather returns, and often the death of the whole plant results.

Wait to lay the pine boughs until the ground begins to freeze. If you put them down too early, they will encourage too much moisture retention—and mice looking for a winter home may move in and will spend the next few months dining on your plants. Christmas trees—which can be had for nothing on December 26—are a convenient source of boughs.

Evergreen boughs serve the same function that snow cover does for plants in the high mountains.

Cut the boughs off the trunks and lay them down in a double overlapping layer, shingling the branches in the second layer over the gaps between branches in the first. Laying the branches down all in one direction will make them easier to remove in the spring.

When the crocuses begin to bloom, remove the top layer of pine boughs to let some light reach the plants. Then, a week or two later, if the weather conditions have not turned unseasonably cold, remove the lower layer. Clean up any dropped needles, carefully picking them out of plant crowns.

One other winter chore is to check periodically for frost heaving in parts of the garden where plants are not protected by pine boughs. If you notice any plants heaved out of the ground, gently heel them back in so their roots are not exposed to cold, drying winds.

Remove accumulations of leaves that have blown in over the winter as soon as possible in late winter.

PESTS IN THE ROCK GARDEN

Rock gardens are not generally subject to the host of ills that afflict perennial borders and other gardens, but some pests can be troublesome. Insect pests may seldom be a problem, but rodents, rabbits, deer, and slugs can cause significant damage.

Besides feeding on your rock plants and bulbs when other food sources are scarce, mice and other rodents may do great harm through their tunneling. They dig through roots, undermine rocks, and destroy any plants that happen to be located at the entrances to their burrows. Often a cat is a sufficient deterrent, but you may have to resort to traps, baits, or even a professional exterminator.

Rabbits may visit the rock garden to graze on the plants there, especially in the winter. Covering the plants with inexpensive (and relatively unobtrusive) plastic netting will discourage them.

Deer do not usually eat little rock plants, but they can trample them with their hooves when passing through the garden on the way to other food sources. Covering plants with netting should persuade the deer to reroute their path.

Slugs love to hide under rocks and organic mulches, and they may even infest gravel mulches. They are especially fond of campanulas. If slugs are the bane of your garden, the first line of defense is to eliminate the organic cover in which they like to hide and breed. Remove fallen leaves and plant debris, and keep the compost pile well away from the garden. Then use beer traps or poisoned baits to clear any slugs already in residence.

Campanulas are especially attractive to slugs—a well-drained soil and a gravel mulch will help discourage them. OPPOSITE: Unobtrusive plastic netting will protect plantings from rabbits and deer.

5

75 GREAT ROCK GARDEN PLANTS

I n this chapter, Robert Bartolomei presents profiles of 75 reliable plants that he recommends as a core planting for a new rock garden. They represent only a small sampler of what is available; even within the genera described below, there may be dozens of species in addition to those covered here. The gentians (*Gentiana* spp.) and the campanulas (*Campanula* spp.), for example, offer a nearly inexhaustible diversity of beautiful plants. As mentioned earlier, experimentation is the watchword of the rock gardener.

Of the plants Bartolomei has chosen to include, most are easy to grow and are well suited to the needs of the ordinary gardener. Some will test horticultural skills and help the reader develop the techniques of an expert rock gardener. To assist in this process, the descriptions offer advice on the soil and type of site preferred by each plant. So that the garden will remain well-stocked, there are also tips on how the various plants should be propagated. If a plant is exceptionally vigorous, and steps must be taken to keep it within bounds, that fact is noted too.

These recommended plants are remarkable for their diversity, and each will make a rewarding addition to the garden.

AETHIONEMA
PERSIAN STONE CRESS, PERSIAN CANDYTUFT

Aethionema grandiflorum, Persian stone cress, is a small, shrubby perennial member of the mustard family. The plant grows about 12 inches high, in a loose, bushy, tufted form. It has slender bluish green leaves to 1 inch long. In mid- to late spring, it bears terminal spikes of small pink flowers the color of strawberry ice cream, each blossom measuring ¼ inch wide.

A. armenum 'Warley Rose', a choice cultivar, is a rather bushy, tufted plant with gnarled, prostrate branches that have ascending tips. It grows just 4 to 6 inches high. Its 1-inch-long, narrow, grayish green leaves are edged faintly with pink. Compact clusters of bright rose-pink flowers bloom in spring. It is propagated from cuttings.

A. oppositifolium, also known as *Eunomia oppositifolia,* is quite different in appearance from other species. It forms a small mat about 8 inches in diameter and only ½ inch tall. Small, rounded, gray-green leaves are borne in pairs along the stems. Heads of fragrant lilac flowers barely emerge above the foliage in early spring. This species is very choice and easy to grow and is suitable for a scree bed or a trough.

Give aethionemas a location in full sun, with light, well-drained soil containing some lime. The plants are drought tolerant and are good choices for a scree bed or stone wall.

Shear back the taller species lightly after blooming to promote bushier growth, unless you want the plants to self-sow.

ALYSSUM SAXATILE
BASKET-OF-GOLD

Now known as *Aurinia saxatilis,* this rock garden standard can also be found in perennial borders. Its brilliant yellow flowers light up the garden in early to mid-spring.

Basket-of-gold is a coarse, tufted plant with soft grayish green, evergreen leaves borne on sprawling stems. The plant grows to about 15 inches high. The cultivar 'Citrina' (opposite) has pale yellow flowers, while those of 'Sunny Border Apricot' (above) are a warm shade of yellow; both hues combine less stridently with other flowering plants than does the golden hue of the species.

Basket-of-gold is drought tolerant and will adapt to a range of soils as long as they are well drained. The stems do not like to rest on moist soil; a gravel mulch is helpful. Give the plant a location in full sun. Deadhead plants when the flowers fade to maintain a neat, compact shape and to keep the plant from bearing masses of self-sown seedlings.

Plant basket-of-gold in a wall or to cascade over a ledge. Propagate the cultivars from cuttings, the species from cuttings or seeds.

ANDROSACE
ROCK JASMINE

Androsaces are related to primulas and count among their number some of the true jewels of the rock garden. Some species pose a considerable challenge to the cultivator, but the following Himalayan natives are both easy to grow and rewarding. *Androsace lanuginosa* is a prostrate plant with a basal rosette of lance-shaped to oval leaves that are covered with silky white hairs and reach a length of up to ¾ inch. In summer, the rosettes elongate to 8 inches long and bear rounded clusters of rose-pink flowers atop slender stems. As in many *Androsace* species, the yellow eye of each flower turns bright cherry red after the insects have visited. This species is valued for its summer flowering. Give *A. lanuginosa* a location where it receives partial shade in summer.

A. sarmentosa (often sold as *A. primuloides*) is a low-growing plant that forms rosettes of oval evergreen leaves

covered with silky white hairs. In late spring, rounded umbels of bright pink flowers bloom atop thin stems as much as 8 inches high. This species spreads much like strawberry plants, by producing offshoots on long, wiry runners. *A. sarmentosa* grows in full sun or partial shade. Well-drained soil, especially near the surface, is important, and a gritty soil mix is best. A gravel mulch provides a dry surface upon which leaves can rest. Good air circulation is essential, especially where summer weather is hot and humid.

Plant these androsaces in a scree or raised bed; the smaller species are suitable for cultivation in troughs. Avoid a scorching southern exposure; northern or eastern is better.

Propagate by pinning the rosettes on runner ends down to the soil and then removing the plantlets after they root.

ANEMONE BLANDA
GRECIAN WINDFLOWER

Anemone blanda is a tuberous-rooted anemone native to the Mediterranean region. It flowers in early to mid-spring at the same time as other hardy bulbs such as narcissus.

Grecian windflower grows about 4 inches high and has finely divided, deep green leaves and many-petaled daisylike flowers. *A. blanda* 'White Splendour' bears flowers of white, rose-backed petals that quiver in the slightest breeze. There are also varieties with pink and blue blossoms, but this white cultivar is larger flowered as well as more vigorous.

Plant this anemone in full sun to partial shade, in fertile, well-drained soil. It likes a location that is rather dry during its summer dormant period.

Grecian windflower is a spring ephemeral suitable for an alpine meadow and other situations in the rock garden. It is especially attractive because, unlike many other bulbs, its foliage does not elongate and become unsightly after it flowers.

AQUILEGIA
COLUMBINE

The smaller species of columbines, with their nodding spurred flowers and scalloped leaves, make graceful additions to the rock garden. *Aquilegia bertolonii* is an especially fine species that reaches a height of 4 to 6 inches, forming a characteristic basal tuft of leaves and short, spurred, blue-violet blossoms. The selection 'Blue Berry' is an easily grown form that bears good blue flowers and is small enough for a trough.

A. *flabellata,* the fanleaf columbine, is a native of Japan that is sometimes seen in herbaceous beds and borders, but it is at its best in the rock garden. It has broad, attractively scalloped leaflets of bluish green and bears short spurred flowers. Unlike most other columbines, this one does not interbreed with other species and so comes true from seed. The cultivar 'Ministar' (often listed as A. *akitensis* 'Ministar') grows about 8 inches high. Its nodding flowers have deep blue-violet sepals that contrast with the cream petals.

A. *f.* 'Nana' (above), usually listed as 'Nana Alba', is a much larger plant that grows to about 12 inches tall and bears drooping white, lavender-blushed flowers in mid- to late spring.

Plant columbines in full sun to partial shade, in well-drained soil. They are not fussy as to pH but do not like to dry out. Mulch with gravel to prevent crown rot.

ARABIS
ROCK CRESS

Arabis caucasica (above) is a long-blooming plant that forms a 5-inch-high mat of spreading stems and heavy, oval and grayish, coarsely toothed leaves. *A. c.* 'Plena' (often sold as 'Flore Plena') produces clusters of double white flowers on 12-inch-tall stems that are more upright than those of other forms of the species; bloom may continue for a month or more in late spring.

Another rock cress, *A. procurrens* 'Variegata' (usually sold as *A. ferdinandi-coburgi* 'Variegata'), has creeping, sprawling stems that form a low mat. The leaves are pointed and glossy deep green; they are edged with white tinged here and there with pink. The plant is dwarfer than the species and forms a ground-hugging mat that blooms rather weakly—actually, the sparse clusters of white flowers are better snipped off as they appear in late spring. A gold-edged selection is also available.

Plant these arabis in full sun to partial shade, in the standard rock garden soil. They are generally easy to grow. *A. caucasica* is attractive if placed where it can drape over a rock or cascade down a slope. Give it plenty of space. *A. procurrens* 'Variegata' is much less aggressive and is a safer option for planting next to smaller, choicer plants.

Propagate new plants from cuttings or by division.

ARENARIA MONTANA
MOUNTAIN SANDWORT

ARMERIA
THRIFT

The mountain sandwort grows to about 8 inches high, forming a loose, open mat of low stems covered with narrow, dark green, evergreen leaves. In early summer, the plant bears beautiful white flowers, each one with a central ovary like a polished jade bead.

Give *Arenaria montana* a spot in full sun with well-drained soil. Plant it in a scree bed or let it cascade from a stone wall. As its name suggests, it is also a good choice for a sand bed.

Propagate new plants from seed.

Armerias are noted for their grayish, evergreen, grassy leaves and the ball-shaped clusters of flowers that emerge atop stems over this foliage in springtime. *Armeria juniperifolia*, syn. *A. caespitosa* (above), is a compact species that grows just 3 inches high, forming a dense, tufted cushion, with grayish needlelike leaves and pink or white flower clusters.

A. maritima, sea thrift, is far more commonly seen and is found in perennial borders as well as rock gardens. Easy to grow and long blooming, sea

ARMERIA
THRIFT

ARUNCUS AETHUSIFOLIUS
KOREAN DWARF GOATSBEARD

thrift can reach a height of 6 to 12 inches. The cultivar 'Dusseldorf Pride' (above) is a compact form that bears bright rose-pink flower heads just above its tuft of green leaves.

Give thrifts of either species a location in full sun. Because of their long taproots, armerias are at home in scree beds, walls, rock crevices, and sand beds. *A. juniperifolia* is small enough for a trough.

Propagate new plants from cuttings taken with a bit of the woody base or from seed.

This fairly recent introduction from Korea is already becoming a favorite of American rock gardeners. About 10 inches tall with fernlike toothed and divided leaves, this species of *Aruncus* bears short but upright panicles of tiny white flowers in late spring, and its appearance is closer to that of an astilbe than to that of its relative, the common perennial goatsbeard, *A. dioicus*.

A. aethusifolius will grow in a sunny spot but looks better in light shade; it requires a well-drained soil. When its needs have been met, it makes a slowly increasing clump that can eventually be divided.

ASARINA PROCUMBENS
CREEPING SNAPDRAGON

ASARUM EUROPAEUM
EUROPEAN WILD GINGER

This trailing plant has long sprawling stems with sticky, kidney-shaped and toothed-edged leaves that are gray-green in color. In summer, it bears tubular, lipped, pale yellow flowers that are similar to those of snapdragons (*Antirrhinum* spp.).

Although not reliably hardy in colder zones, creeping snapdragon will reestablish itself year after year by means of self-sown seedlings. It often sows itself into narrow crevices and is a beautiful addition to a planted wall. This plant also thrives in dry shade, a type of location that is not hospitable to many other rock plants. Easily started from seed, creeping snapdragon may also be propagated from cuttings.

A lovely mat-forming ground cover, *Asarum europaeum* is a good choice for a woodland or other shady rock garden. Its glossy, heart-shaped leaves spring from creeping stems and are evergreen where winters are not too harsh. The jug-shaped flowers are brownish in color and hidden under the foliage.

European wild ginger needs shade and a moist, fertile soil. Propagate new plants by division.

AUBRIETA × CULTORUM
PURPLE ROCK CRESS

BOLAX GUMMIFERA

The Latin name indicates that any aubrietas sold under this label are of hybrid origin; many of the plants sold as *A. deltoidea* actually belong in this group, and there are many cultivars.

In general, these plants form evergreen cushions covered with four-petaled, violet to dark red flowers that open over a long season in the spring. Although these aubrietas are most at home in a sunny eastern exposure, they will tolerate some shade. Aubrietas adapt well to soils with a higher (neutral to alkaline) pH and are very tolerant of drought. Vigorous specimens should be sheared back after flowering to maintain compactness.

When planted into a situation that suits them, these are long-lived plants. An excellent choice for walls, crevices, and scree and sand beds, aubrietas may be grown from seed, or from cuttings taken in the fall. They may also be propagated by division.

A curiosity for adventurous rock gardeners, *Bolax gummifera* 'Nana' (syn. *B. glebaria*) grows to a height of less than an inch and forms a neat cushion of tiny, three-lobed, glossy deep green leaves that slowly expand into large mats. Though this plant bears insignificant yellow flowers, it is grown primarily for its glossy, almost artificial-looking foliage.

The leaves will scorch in hot, dry conditions, so plant bolax on an eastern exposure or where it will get some protection from the afternoon sun. The species is native to the southern tip of South America and is perfectly hardy throughout the northern United States. Plant it in the standard rock garden soil mix where it will not dry out. Propagate new plants by division.

CAMPANULA
BELLFLOWER

Campanulas are favorites among gardeners, and many are wonderfully suited to the rock garden.

Campanula carpatica, Carpathian bellflower, is a low-growing campanula that forms a mat of oval, 1½-inch-long leaves. In summer, it produces an abundance of bell-shaped, blue-violet flowers 1½ to 2 inches wide. It is valued for its late flowering.

C. cochleariifolia (syn. *C. pusilla*), or fairy's thimble, is a small but vigorous species from the Alps. Its slender runners travel underground, sending up 2-inch tufts of glossy, rounded leaves.

The wiry flowering stems reach a height of 6 inches and bear perfect nodding ½-inch bells of lavender, violet, or near white.

C. poscharskyana, Serbian bellflower, is a vigorous trailer whose long stems stay close to the ground but which may reach a length of 15 inches. This species' pale green, kidney-shaped leaves grow to 1½ inches long, and in summertime the plants bear star-shaped flowers of pale lavender-blue.

Dalmatian bellflower or wall bellflower, *C. portenschlagiana,* formerly *C. muralis* (above), is an easily cultivated

CAMPANULA
BELLFLOWER

species that grows about 6 inches high and has a tufted habit, bearing kidney-shaped leaves that are hidden by a mass of blue-violet bells in early summer.

Most campanulas grow best in full sun to partial shade and in well-drained soil of average fertility. Many, however, will also grow in ordinary well-drained garden soil. *C. poschar-skyana* is drought resistant and prefers partial shade. It is too invasive for the carefully tended rock garden but useful for an alpine meadow or anywhere else where it can be allowed to romp.

C. carpatica self-sows readily and for this reason occasionally becomes a problem in small rock gardens. Generally, though, it is worth the extra work it might cause.

C. portenschlagiana (above) is an excellent, long-lasting wall or crevice plant.

C. cochleariifolia is a natural choice for a scree bed, where its underground stems enable it to appear and disappear at will.

Propagate new plants by division or from seed. You can easily move self-sown seedlings to other parts of the garden.

CORYDALIS LUTEA

A lovely plant for a shady rock garden, *Corydalis lutea* has attractive ferny green leaves; it bears clusters of small, nodding, bright yellow flowers throughout much of the summer. It has a tufted habit and reaches a height of about 16 inches. Corydalis self-sows freely and spreads itself about the garden, showing a special preference for crevices. It is also a good choice for a planted wall.

Plants may be propagated from seed, but this requires patience since the seeds can take as long as 2 years to germinate. It is best to sow them while still fresh right in the spot where you hope to have them flower. Once even a single plant has established itself in your garden, however, you are sure to see many others before long. Indeed, they can overwhelm less vigorous neighbors, so be conscientious about removing unwanted seedlings.

CROCUS

Species crocuses bring color to sunny areas of the rock garden in early spring or fall. Bulb catalogs offer a wide selection. The chalice-shaped flowers are followed by narrow, grassy leaves, and these must not be cut back until they yellow and wither, for it is this year's foliage that makes the food for next year's bloom. Keep this in mind when placing crocuses within the garden, and do not put them anywhere that the persistent leaves can become a problem.

Crocuses also need a well-drained soil that is reasonably fertile and that does not remain overly moist during their summer dormancy. All in all, an alpine meadow is the best part of the rock garden for them.

Crocus speciosus, often called showy autumn crocus, bears flowers in shades of lavender or white with bright orange stigmas. Plants spread easily through the garden and are relatively squirrel proof. This species flowers in October, though the foliage appears in spring.

C. tommasinianus, tommy crocus, is an early-spring bloomer with lilac or white flowers. It grows best where the soil gets some shade during the day. Although it can become somewhat of a pest in the rock garden, it is suggested here where a squirrel-proof spring crocus is desired.

CYCLAMEN COUM

DELOSPERMA NUBIGENUM
HARDY ICE PLANT

Hardy cyclamens are among the greatest treasures of the rock garden. Their heart-shaped leaves and shooting-star flowers with reflexed petals give them a charm all their own.

Cyclamen coum is among the hardier species and will overwinter successfully through zone 5. It grows just 4 inches high, bearing chubby pink or white flowers during warm spells in winter and into early spring. The leaves are streaked with silvery white. It is beautiful when planted in combination with snowdrops (*Galanthus* spp.).

Plant *C. coum* in a woodland or a shaded spot in the rock garden where the soil is well drained but rich in organic matter. Hardy cyclamens grow from tubers, and those of *C. coum* should be planted with the tuber's top level with the soil surface. New plants are easily started from seed—ants will often do the job of sowing the seed for you.

This ice plant, which comes from the colder mountains of South Africa, is surprisingly hardy. It quickly forms a broad mat of fleshy medium green leaves that in springtime covers itself with bright yellow, narrow-petaled flowers that measure an inch across. An unusual and distinctive succulent, it is hardiest when planted into a well-drained scree. It is easy to propagate from cuttings or by division.

DIANTHUS
PINK

The pinks (*Dianthus* spp.) are mostly mat- or cushion-forming plants with narrow, grayish green leaves that bear flowers with fringed petals of pink, red, or white. There are a host of smaller species and cultivars that make delightful additions to the rock garden.

D. alpinus (above left) has blunt-ended, dark green leaves, and in late spring it produces broad rosy pink blossoms with a red central ring atop short stems. Some cultivars have white ('Albus', above right) or dark red blossoms. As its name implies, this is a native of the Alps. This species requires a scree that is relatively rich in soil and that never dries out completely; *D. alpinus* also needs at least a half day of sun. Propagate new plants from cuttings or by division.

D. deltoides, the maiden pink, is easy to grow. The species form bears masses of small magenta-pink flowers, but there are cultivars that produce blossoms in shades of pink, red, and white, sometimes with a contrasting stripe. This species self-sows and will spread quickly if you let it. Maiden pink is a good choice for an alpine meadow, but keep it well away from choicer plants.

D. gratianopolitanus (syn. *D. caesius*),

DIANTHUS
PINK

the Cheddar pink (above left and right), covers itself in early summer with rose-pink flowers of a spicy-sweet clove fragrance. The blue-green, grassy leaves form a dense mat. In the garden, this species is known through its cultivars and hybrids; the best forms for the rock garden are those with short flowering stems and single blossoms. Grow cheddar pink in a stone wall or on a rock ledge.

D. pavonius (syn. *D. neglectus*), the glacier pink, is a cushion plant that grows to a height of 6 inches, bearing evergreen grassy leaves and pink, green-eyed flowers. The undersides of the petals are a distinctive buff color. It is a choice species and very reliable in a scree bed or trough.

D. 'Tiny Rubies' is a petite plant of hybrid origin; its tiny double blossoms of pale pink are exceptionally appealing.

Most dianthus species are deep-rooted plants that like well-drained, limy soil and plenty of sun. Good drainage is an essential protection against crown rot, to which these plants are prone. They are generally easy to grow.

Propagate the species from seed, the hybrids and cultivars from cuttings.

DRABA
WHITLOW GRASS

Drabas, with the exception of a few touchy species that are usually grown in alpine houses, are very easy and useful plants for the rock garden.

Draba aizoides, with its tufts of bright yellow flowers, is one of earliest plants to bloom in the rock garden. It forms a 6-inch cushion of pointed evergreen leaves edged in fine hairs and is a drought-tolerant plant well adapted to crevices and screes.

A vigorous trailer, _D. sibirica_ sends long stems meandering along the ground from a central rosette of hairy, light green leaves. The stems put down roots and the plant eventually forms a mat. In spring, the plants produce clusters of bright mustard yellow flowers on 6-inch stems. Extremely hardy and easy to grow, it is a good choice for a ledge or an alpine meadow.

Plant drabas in full sun to light shade, and in a soil that is gritty and well drained but that contains some organic matter. Propagate new plants from seed for all species, by division for _D. sibirica,_ and from cuttings for _D. aizoides._

EPIMEDIUM
BARRENWORT

ERINUS ALPINUS
FAIRY FOXGLOVE

Epimediums make fine ground covers for shady gardens. An outstanding cultivar is *Epimedium* X *youngianum* 'Niveum', which bears pure white flowers in late spring and has the elegant compound leaves typical of the genus. 'Niveum' is also one of the dwarfest of the barrenworts, growing to a height of only 8 inches or so.

Plant epimediums in shady areas of the rock garden, in well-drained soil. They are drought tolerant once established.

Propagate new plants by division of crowded clumps soon after plants finish blooming.

A European native, *Erinus alpinus* forms a neat, 4-inch mound of rich green leaves with toothed edges. The species form bears clusters of small rosy purple blossoms in late spring, but there is also a white-flowered form that is commonly available.

Plant *E. alpinus* in full sun to partial shade; it thrives best in a scree mix, since excess moisture and fertility causes the center of the plant to rot. It is a good plant for crevices and walls, and though not long lived, it self-sows. It can also be propagated from cuttings.

EUPHORBIA MYRSINITES
SPURGE

A trailing member of a large and varied genus, *Euphorbia myrsinites* grows well in the rock garden. It has thick bluish green leaves and in spring bears inconspicuous flowers surrounded by ornamental yellow bracts.

Grow this euphorbia where a larger plant is called for; it flourishes in full sun on outcrops or ledges where the stems can trail over the rocks.

Propagate new plants from seed, or move self-sown seedlings to spots where you want them to grow. Trim off old stems to improve the plant's appearance after flowering.

GENTIANA
GENTIAN

The gentians, with their lovely blue blossoms, are classic rock garden plants. Many species are demanding in their cultural requirements, and growing them successfully is a challenge to the gardener's skills. But they are worth the effort, for these plants are irresistibly delightful in bloom.

There are many gentians, enough species to fill an entire garden, but those described here are especially well suited to the beginning rock gardener.

Trumpet gentian, *Gentiana acaulis,* is native to the Swiss Alps. It produces dense tufts of deep green leaves and, in late spring, impressively large, blue, trumpet-shaped blossoms with beautiful green-spotted throats—these may measure 3 inches long.

Rough gentian, *G. scabra,* is a taller, upright plant with stems to 1 foot high and oval leaves. Its dark blue flowers appear in autumn at the ends of the stems. It will grow in moist to average soil and where happy will self-sow.

G. septemfida is extremely hardy and reaches a height of about 1 foot. It has oval leaves and in summer bears at the ends of its stems clusters of bell-shaped, deep blue blossoms with white throats.

GENTIANA
GENTIAN

It is the most dependable of gentians.

Spring gentian, *G. verna* (opposite), grows just 3 inches high, forming a small, tufted mat. In spring, it bears small, clear blue flowers with white eyes. This is a difficult species to grow in the garden; the form available as *G. v.* var. *angulosa* appears to be the easiest to cultivate successfully.

Give gentians a sunny location, with a bit of shade during the hottest part of the day. A cool, northern exposure, such as the unobstructed north side of a slope, is ideal. Gentians need humusy, well-drained, evenly moist soil.

They benefit from yearly additions of compost or aged cow manure to the soil immediately around their roots—some gardeners have substituted timed-release fertilizers with great success.

Most gentians have long taproots, and these make them difficult to transplant. Once established, most gentians should be left undisturbed; notable exceptions to this rule are *G. verna* and *G. acaulis,* which should be lifted and divided every third or fourth year, or when flowering seems to decline. Propagate new plants from fresh seed.

GERANIUM
CRANESBILL

Hardy geraniums, called cranesbills because of the long, narrow shape of their seed capsules, have long found a home in perennial beds and borders. Many of the popular species are too large for the rock garden, but there are smaller cranesbills that are well adapted to use there.

Geranium cinereum 'Ballerina', ashy cranesbill, is a tufted plant that grows about 6 inches high and has palmately divided, gray-green leaves. It bears lavender-pink flowers marked with deep pink veins over a long season in summer.

G. dalmaticum, Dalmatian cranesbill (above left and opposite) is a bushy, mat-forming plant that grows 6 inches high and 1 to 1½ feet across. It has green palmate leaves and light pink flowers. The cultivar 'Album' is an especially beautiful form with white flowers blushed pink.

G. sanguineum var. *striatum* (above right), known as Lancaster geranium (formerly listed as *G. s.* var. *lancastriense*), is a vigorous mat-forming plant that grows to 6 inches tall. Its finely divided palmate leaves are grayish green, and the flowers, which bloom well into summer, are a lovely clear pink with darker pink veins.

Hardy geraniums grow best in full sun to light shade. Give 'Ballerina' a very well drained, limy, gritty soil. A scree suits it best. Dalmatian and Lancaster geraniums need soil that is a bit richer, and they grow well in standard rock garden mix.

Geraniums are versatile plants for screes, raised beds, crevices and walls, or alpine meadows.

GLOBULARIA CORDIFOLIA
HEARTLEAF GLOBE DAISY

GYPSOPHILA REPENS
CREEPING BABY'S BREATH

Heartleaf globe daisy is aptly described by its common name. Growing only 2 inches high, it forms a neat, ground-covering mat of tiny, leathery, heart-shaped leaves. In summer, it bears small, fluffy, globe-shaped heads of tiny, light blue blossoms.

An excellent and long-lived scree plant, *Globularia cordifolia* prefers a light, well-drained soil that contains some lime, although it tolerates other soils as well. A location in full sun, with rocks over which the stems may drape themselves, is ideal.

Propagate new plants from cuttings or by division.

Gypsophila repens is a vigorous mat-forming perennial that bears airy, white to pale pink panicles of blossoms in summer. Complementing the bloom are the attractive, narrow, grayish green leaves.

Give creeping baby's breath a location in full sun, with well-drained soil —preferably, one with a mildly alkaline pH.

This plant is a good choice for screes, crevices and walls, or even an alpine meadow.

Propagate new plants from cuttings or seed.

HYPERICUM OLYMPICUM
ST. JOHN'S WORT

Hypericum olympicum is a low, tufted shrub, each of its yellow flowers filled with cluster of long stamens that seem to capture and distill the bright summer sun. It reaches a height of about 1 foot and has narrow, grayish green leaves. The cultivar 'Citrinum' has blossoms of a softer shade of yellow than the golden-flowered species.

Give *H. olympicum* a sunny location with well-drained soil. It is very drought tolerant once established and will thrive in a scree, on a ledge or outcrop, or in crevices and walls. Shear it back lightly after flowering to maintain a compact shape.

Propagate new plants by division or from cuttings.

LEWISIA COTYLEDON
SISKIYOU BITTERROOT

Relatives of the portulaca, lewisias are among the most coveted of American rock plants. This species, a native to the Siskiyou Mountains of northern California and southern Oregon, was once heavily collected, but today *Lewisia cotyledon* is usually grown in its cultivated forms. Several different strains and cultivars are commonly available.

L. cotyledon is among the easier species to grow as well as one of the showiest. It forms a rosette of long, succulent, evergreen leaves that are a rich green in hue and often have fluted edges. In late spring or early summer, clusters of lovely apricot, orange, pink, white, or striped and two-toned flowers appear atop slender, branched stems about 6 inches tall.

Lewisias must have excellent drainage if they are to escape crown rot. A crevice is an ideal spot, but a scree bed is also a good place for them, and surrounding them with a gravel mulch is advisable. Applications of fertilizer are needed if the plants are to flower dependably when growing on lean scree soils. Lewisias do not like lime, and they prefer a somewhat acid soil.

Siting is a key to success with lewisias. Despite their succulent appearance, they require a location in partial shade, and a cool northern or perhaps eastern exposure is ideal.

MINUARTIA LARICIFOLIA
LARCHLEAF SANDWORT

NARCISSUS

Minuartia laricifolia (syn. *Arenaria larici-folia*) is a low, handsome, mat-forming ground cover with small, needlelike leaves that bears masses of pure white flowers in early summer. The stems creep along the ground and root as they go.

Plant larchleaf sandwort in full sun, in well-drained soil. Scree beds and rocky ledges and sand beds suit them well.

Propagate new plants by division or from seed.

There are many dwarf narcissus suitable for the rock garden, but one of the most delightful and unusual is the hoop-petticoat daffodil, *Narcissus bulbocodium* var. *conspicuus*. It grows to a height of about 15 inches, and the yellow flowers have a flared cup suggestive of its namesake.

Hoop-petticoat and other small narcissus and daffodils are charming when set in alpine meadows, although the very smallest species should be grown in clumps on ledges where they may be more easily appreciated.

Give narcissus full sun to partial shade and well-drained soil. The hoop petticoat thrives in sandy acidic soil.

PAPAVER ALPINUM
ALPINE POPPY

As fragile as it appears, the alpine poppy is a tough little plant.

Wild alpine poppies have been separated into several species by botanists, but the plant discussed here is the cultivated seed strain that appears under this name, which is probably a hybrid of several species. Six inches above a tuft of finely divided, bluish green leaves arise four-petaled flowers of tissue-paper substance on wiry stems. The color range is white to yellow, pastel pinks to warm orange.

Poppies can be difficult to transplant, so sprinkle the seed directly onto the garden in spring. They thrive in any sunny spot where they are not crowded by other plants.

**PARONYCHIA KAPELA SSP.
SERPYLLIFOLIA** *NAILWORT*

PETRORHAGIA SAXIFRAGA
TUNIC FLOWER

This is a small plant that likes hot, dry conditions. Growing less than ½ inch high, it forms a low mat of tiny leaves. Its inconspicuous flowers are surrounded by silvery bracts that glimmer through much of the summer.

Nailwort needs excellent drainage, and the sprawling stems will spread tightly over rocks or form a carpet over a gravel mulch. It has a surprisingly deep and wiry root system, which makes it an excellent soil-binding ground cover for spots where the slope is steep and tends to erode. Give the plants full sun. This is a very dependable plant. Indeed, the mat it forms will require cutting back if it is set beside less aggressive neighbors.

Propagate by division or from seed.

Formerly classified as *Tunica saxifraga,* this plant is a wiry, airy, mat-forming species that may reach a height of 10 inches. It has needlelike dark green leaves and many tiny summer flowers of white or pink. The cultivar 'Rosette' has double pink flowers that appear all through the summer.

Give the tunic flower a location in full sun, with well-drained soil. If it begins to look ragged, give it a mid-summer shearing—it recovers quickly.

Propagate new plants by division or from cuttings. The single form will self-sow.

PHLOX

The phloxes are a diverse and lovely clan of American natives. Some are perfect for cutting gardens, others are at home in woodlands—many are ideal for the rock garden.

Moss phlox or moss pink, *Phlox subulata* (above left), is a mat-forming evergreen ground cover that bursts into brilliant bloom in early spring. The plants have needlelike leaves and flowers in shades of pink, lavender, red, and blue as well as white.

There are many cultivars that are superior in color, vigor, and habit to those usually sold in local garden centers. Three worthy of note are 'Crackerjack', a dwarf that bears brilliant red flowers and is suitable for a scree or a trough; 'Amazing Grace', a normal-sized form with soft white, pink-eyed flowers; and 'White Delight', which blooms a shimmering white. The subspecies *brittonii* ('Green Ridge', above right) has a compact, cushiony form and is an especially good plant for a scree. It bears white to pale pink flowers with deeply notched petals.

Moss phlox is adaptable and easy to

PHLOX

grow. It loves the sun and loose, well-drained rock garden soil or scree.

Moss phlox can be planted on ledges, and the more vigorous forms do well in alpine meadow. The compact forms, often labeled *P. X douglasii,* are suitable for crevices, screes, and troughs, where they flourish in combination with plants of similar scale.

The cleft or sand phlox, *P. bifida* (above left and right), is less commonly available but is well worth seeking out. It is a looser, more open plant than *P. subulata* and grows to a height of about 10 inches. The foliage is longer and broader, so that the whole appearance is somewhat coarse. This species is, however, a standout during its spring bloom, when it covers itself with relatively large flowers, the petals of which are deeply cut and notched, giving the appearance of lavender or white snowflakes. It is not as moisture tolerant as *P. subulata,* so it is best planted in scree or in a sand bed in regions of abundant summer rainfall.

PRIMULA × _PRUHONICIANA_
PRIMROSE

If you live in a cool, moist climate, the kind of climate that suits primroses best, you will find that there are hundreds of species and varieties from which to choose. If, however, you worry that your rock garden might prove less than hospitable, you should at least try the so-called Juliana primroses, an undemanding strain of *Primula* X *pruhoniciana* hybrids. Of these, the hardiest cultivars seem to be those that are vegetatively propagated, such as 'Wanda', which has deep purple flowers and dark foliage; 'Lois Lutz', whose flowers are a brilliant cerise; and 'Dorothy', whose blossoms are a classic pale, primrose yellow.

These are not only relatively hardy but also compact. They begin flowering as the foliage emerges in spring and continue their bloom over several weeks. They grow best in those areas of the rock garden where they get afternoon shade and in soil that is rich and moisture retentive but not soggy. An annual fertilization is required, and established plants should be lifted and divided every third year. Alternate freezing and thawing of the soil in winter may loosen and heave these shallow-rooted plants, but this can be fixed by gently firming the root balls back into the soil.

PULSATILLA VULGARIS
PASQUEFLOWER

RAMONDA MYCONI

Early in spring, the pasqueflower opens its flowers: the flower stems emerge even before the leaves, bearing large blossoms with silky petals and yellow stamens. The flowers are purple in the species form; the seed strain 'Papageno' flowers are pink, red and white, or violet. Its petals are deeply cut like parrot feathers.

The feathery plumed seed heads that replace the flowers are attractive, too, as are the finely divided leaves that sprout in tufted basal rosettes about 10 inches high. All in all, this plant is hard to resist, although it verges on being too large for many situations.

Pasqueflower likes full sun or very light shade, and a very well drained, not too fertile soil, ideally with a somewhat alkaline pH. If possible, sow seed directly where you want the plants to grow; they have a long taproot and do not transplant well. Grow pasqueflower on a scree bed or on drier ledges.

This species is a hardy relative of the African violets and other gesneriads that are so popular as houseplants. Like its relatives, *Ramonda myconi* produces a rosette of hairy, oval leaves that lie close to the ground; in early summer, it bears clusters of five-petaled, lavender-blue flowers on upright 4- to 6-inch stems. At the center of each flower is a cluster of golden stamens, and running around this, through the base of the petals, is a yellow ring.

Site ramonda along an outcrop or in a crevice or wall. These plants like a well-drained soil containing some humus; they are drought tolerant and are prone to rot if stuck in a wet spot. A northern or northeastern exposure is crucial to successful cultivation of this beautiful and unusual plant.

Propagate new plants by division of old crowns or from seed.

SAPONARIA
SOAPWORT

Soapworts got their common name from the fact that when mixed with water some species' leaves produce a cleansing lather—at one time soapwort was used by the textile industry to wash woolens. Today the smaller species are valued as easily grown, free-blooming additions to the rock garden.

Rock soapwort, *Saponaria ocymoides* (above), forms a spreading mat of deep green leaves that is covered with purple-pink flowers in late spring. This plant makes a beautiful sight tumbling over rocks or cascading from a wall, but it is an aggressive spreader and can become a pest when it is near smaller plants. The white form is also attractive.

S. X *olivana* is better behaved—not invasive—and bears pinkish lavender flowers that open in a wheel-like fashion around its 6-inch cushion of foliage. It comes true from seed.

S. 'Bressingham Hybrid' (opposite) is a choice mat-forming plant that grows only 1 inch tall and bears eye-catching, bright rose flowers. It is propagated from cuttings.

Grow saponarias in full sun, in a scree mix or other coarse, well-drained soil. Soapworts take well to planting in walls, and the last two plants described above are suitable for troughs.

SAXIFRAGA
SAXIFRAGE

Every rock garden needs some sax-ifrages. That's an easy condition to ful-fill, too, since this large and varied genus offers many choices, and the dif-ferent species adapt to a wide range of conditions. Three excellent species are described here.

Saxifraga X *apiculata* (opposite) is a member of the Porphyrion section of the saxifrages, a group that includes many choice plants, some of which are challenging to grow in the open gar-den. This species, however, is easy. It produces a mat of rosettes of dark green, pointed leaves and bears clusters of yellow flowers in mid-spring. It requires light shade and a well-drained soil that does not dry out.

Another group of species is the "encrusted" saxifrages; this group gets its name from the white crusty deposits of lime that form along the edges of the plants' leaves, creating a silvery effect. These leaves are spatula shaped with toothed edges and are gathered into rosettes. The rosettes of the species *S. cotyledon* (above) measure up to 8 inches across, with oblong, untoothed leaves and clusters of white flowers atop stems as long as 2 feet. Each plant's original rosette dies after flowering, but new ones are produced alongside it.

S. paniculata is of more modest pro-portions, reaching a height of about 10 inches when in bloom; this stalk sends out clusters of white, pale pink, or pale yellow flowers on slender stems from 2- to 3-inch-wide rosettes in early summer. Both *S. cotyledon* and *S. paniculata* spread by means of offsets.

These saxifrages need well-drained, gritty soil, but they cannot tolerate drought. In hot, dry weather, they need careful watering. Plant them in partial shade, in a scree bed or crevice.

Propagate the encrusted saxifrages by division of offsets. Propagate *S.* X *apiculata* from cuttings.

SEMPERVIVUM
HOUSELEEK

These popular plants are known as hens-and-chickens, because they reproduce by offsets; they are also sometimes called houseleeks, because in Europe they were once commonly found growing on rooftops. An endless number of cultivars have been produced in the United States, and these offer many unusual forms, colors, and variations in size.

One of the most interesting is the cobweb houseleek, *Sempervivum arachnoideum,* which grows in a rosette of thick, pointed, oval leaves whose tips are connected by a web of white hairs. Mature rosettes expand upward to produce a cluster of salmon to rosy pink flowers in summer.

Sempervivums are durable plants that thrive in sandy or gritty soil of average to poor fertility. They require good drainage and are happiest in a spot that receives shade for part of the day. Their roots will take hold in a small pocket of soil in a crevice or wall, and they can adhere right onto a rock, if the rock is soft enough to retain some moisture.

Plant sempervivums in crevices or walls, on ledges, or in scree beds.

Propagate new plants by division of offsets.

SILENE SCHAFTA

THYMUS
THYME

A relative of the campions or catchflies, *Silene schafta* sends forth its bright magenta flowers in late summer when little else is blooming in the garden. Its 6- to 10-inch stems form a tufted mat covered with slender, hairy green leaves.

This plant grows in practically any ordinary soil that is not too moist, so long as the plants get plenty of sun— *S. schafta* is easy to grow in a scree bed or on a dry ledge. Individual plants may not be long-lived, but a planting will perpetuate itself by self-sowing.

Propagate by division, from cuttings, from or seed.

Their combination of fragrance, texture, and flowers makes the creeping thymes some of the very best rock garden plants. One of Robert Bartolomei's favorites is *Thymus praecox* ssp. *arcticus* (which is commonly sold under the name *T. serpyllum*). A native of Scandinavia and Greenland, this thyme is reliably hardy in the northern U.S. states and has hairy stems that creep along the ground bearing small oval leaves and, in summer, clusters of tiny rose-purple flowers. The form 'Albus' is especially dwarf and floriferous and produces pale green leaves and pure white flowers; 'Coccineus' is low growing and has dark foliage and bright red-purple flowers.

Creeping thymes are excellent for planting between paving stones in a path, in a wall, or as ground cover in an alpine meadow. They appreciate plenty of sun and well-drained soil, and are drought tolerant.

VERONICA
SPEEDWELL

This genus is well known for the pretty flowers it contributes to perennial beds and borders, but the veronicas are well represented in rock gardens, too. There are many choice species—those described here are just a sampling.

Veronica spicata 'Nana' is a true dwarf that forms mats of foliage only 1 inch tall, but it covers itself with 2- to 3-inch spikes of fuzzy blue flowers in early summer.

V. pectinata is another prostrate, mat-forming plant; it has pale, toothed leaves and in late spring bears many short spikes of deep blue flowers with white eyes. An Asian native, this species is extremely hardy.

Veronicas will thrive in any standard rock garden soil mix. A location in full sun to partial shade suits them just fine.

These veronicas are at home on ledges or in alpine meadows.

Propagate new plants by division.

APPENDIX A: SOURCES FOR ROCK GARDEN PLANTS

CALIFORNIA	COLORADO	COLORADO
NANCY R. WILSON SPECIES & MINIATURE NARCISSUS 6525 Briceland-Thorn Road Garberville, CA 95542 (707) 923-2407	**ALPLAINS SEED CATALOG** 32315 Pine Crest Court Kiowa, CO 80117	**LAPORTE AVENUE NURSERY** Kirk Fieseler 1950 Laporte Avenue Fort Collins, CO 80521
Featuring bulbs from James S. Wells's collection	Alpine plants	Rocky Mountain alpines, western High Plains plants, and rock garden plants

COLORADO	COLORADO	MONTANA
MARTY AND SANDY JONES COLORADO ALPINES, INC. P.O. Box 2708 Avon, CO 81620 (303) 949-6464	**ROCKY MOUNTAIN RARE PLANTS** P.O. Box 200483 Denver, CO 80220	**CHEHALIS RARE PLANT NURSERY** 19081 Julie Road Lebanon, MO 65536 Attn: Herb Dickson
	Wild collected and cultivated seed of cushion and saxatile plants	Auricula seeds, exhibition alpines, hand-pollinated double auricula

NORTH CAROLINA	NORTH CAROLINA	NEW JERSEY
CAMELLIA FOREST NURSERY 125 Carolina Forest Road Chapel Hill, NC 27516	**WE-DU NURSERIES** Rte. 5, Box 724 Marion, NC 28752-9338 (704) 738-8300	**THE CUMMINS GARDEN** 22 Robertsville Road Marlboro, NJ 07746 (908) 536-2591
Hardy camillias, dwarf conifers, rare asian trees and shrubs	American and Asiatic wildflowers, unusual perennials, rockery plants, species iris and daylilies, ferns and fern relatives, hardy and tender bulbs	Dwarf rhododendrons, deciduous azaleas, dwarf evergreens, companion plants

NORTH AMERICAN ROCK GARDEN SOCIETY
Jacques Mommens,
Executive Secretary
P.O. Box 67
Millwood, NY 10546

ROSLYN NURSERY
211 Burrs Lane, Dept. R
Dix Hills, NY 11746

TRENNOLL NURSERY
Jim and Dorothy Parker
3 West Page Avenue
Trenton, OH 45067-1614
(513) 988-6121

Over 1,500 hard-to-find,
useful varieties

Unusual rock plants,
shade plants, hosts,
perennials, geraniums,
iris species, phlox species,
succulents, thymes,
wildflowers, and seed list

NATURE'S GARDEN
40611 Hwy. 226
Scio, OR 97374-9351
(503) 394-3217

PORTERHOWSE
41370 S.E. Thomas Road
Sandy, OR 97055
(503) 668-5834 phone/fax

SISKIYOU RARE PLANT NURSERY
Dept. 1
2825 Cummings Road
Medford, OR 97501
(503) 772-6846

Iris: Siberians, Japanese,
species; primula: julianas,
candelabras, japonicas;
bog plants; pulmonarias

Rare and dwarf conifers,
unique broadleafs, alpine and
rock garden perennials

Over 1,000 varieties of
alpines, ferns, dwarf conifers,
Northwest natives, and
other hardy plants

**HANSEN NURSERY
ROBIN L. HANSEN**
P.O. Box 446
Donald, OR 97020
(503) 678-5409

JOY CREEK NURSERY
20300 N.W. Watson Road
Bin 1
Scappoose, OR 97056

LEWISIA
Rare Plant Research
13245 S.E. Harold
Portland, OR 97236
(503) 762-0289 fax

Species cyclamen grown from
cultivated stock

1,000 hardy perennials,
including penstemons,
dianthus, salvias, and
Northwest natives

22 species and hybrids,
with a variety of flower colors

PENNSYLVANIA	PENNSYLVANIA	SOUTH CAROLINA
DILWORTH NURSERY R-1200 Election Road Oxford, PA 19363 (610) 932-0347 phone (610) 932-9057 fax	**THE PRIMROSE PATH** R.D. 2, Box 110 Scottsdale, PA 15683 (412) 887-6756	**WOODLANDERS** Dept. RG 1128 Colleton Avenue Aiken, SC 29801
Propagators and growers of a large selection of dwarf and unusual conifers and woody ornamental plants	Choice and unusual perennials, alpines, woodland plants, all nursery propagated; new hybrids, species primulas and phlox, native wildflowers, western plants adaptable to the East	Nursery-grown trees, shrubs, perennials, southern natives and exotics

WASHINGTON	ENGLAND	ENGLAND
MOUNT TAHOMA NURSERY Rick Lupp 28111-112th Avenue E. Graham, WA 98338 (206) 847-9827	**POTTERTON & MARTIN** Nettleton Nr. Caistor North Lincs LN7 6HX England (01144) 1472-851792 phone/fax	**THE ALPINE GARDEN SOCIETY** AGS Centre Avon Bank Pershore, Worcester WR10 3JP England
Alpines, Washington State natives, species primulas, troughs and trough plants, dwarf shrubs	Collectors' dwarf bulbs, numerous rare and new introductions, many old favorites for garden and alpine house	

GERMANY	SCOTLAND	SOUTH AFRICA
JELITTO PERENNIAL SEEDS P.O. Box 1264 D-29685 Schwarmstedt, Germany (01149) 5071-4085 phone (01149) 5071-4088 fax	**SCOTTISH ROCK GARDEN CLUB** Contact: Mrs. J. Thomlinson 1, Hillcrest Road Bearsden, Glasgow G61 2EB	**SILVERHILL SEEDS** P.O. Box 53108 Kenilworth 7745 Cape Town South Africa (2721) 762-4245 phone (2721) 797-6609 fax
		Collectors and distributors of seeds of over 2,000 species of native South African plants

APPENDIX B:
A GUIDE TO
PUBLIC ROCK
GARDENS

*Visitors should phone ahead
for information on fees and hours
open to the public, or to schedule
appointments, if necessary.*

CALIFORNIA

HUNTINGTON BOTANICAL GARDEN
1151 Oxford Road
San Marino, CA 91108
(818) 405-2160

COLORADO

DENVER BOTANIC GARDENS
909 York Street
Denver, CO 80206
(303) 331-4000

BETTY FORD ALPINE GARDEN
183 Gore Creek Drive
Vail, CO 81657
(303) 476-0103

CONNECTICUT

ELIZABETH PARK
Department of Parks
and Recreation
25 Stonington Street
Hartford, CT 06106
(203) 722-6541

FLORIDA

KANAPAHA BOTANICAL GARDEN
North Florida Botanical Society
4625 S.W. 63rd Boulevard
Gainesville, FL 32608
(904) 372-4981

GEORGIA

STATE BOTANICAL GARDEN OF GEORGIA
2450 South Milledge Avenue
Athens, GA 30605
(404) 542-1244

MASSACHUSETTS

BOTANIC GARDEN OF SMITH COLLEGE
Lyman Plant House
Northhampton, MA 01063
(413) 585-2748

MICHIGAN

FERNWOOD BOTANIC GARDEN
1720 Range Line Road
Niles, MI 49120
(616) 695-6491 or 695-6688

MINNESOTA

LAKE HARRIET ROCK GARDEN
Lyndale Park and Garden Center
Minneapolis, MN
(612) 348-2142

SIBLEY GARDENS
Parklane and Given Street
Mankato, MN 56001
(507) 625-3161

MISSOURI

WOODLAND AND FLORAL GARDENS
I-43 Agriculture Building
University of Missouri
Columbia, MO 65211
(314) 882-7511

NEVADA

WILBER D. MAY ARBORETUM
Rancho San Rafael Park
1502 Washington Street
Reno, NV 89502
(702) 785-4153

NEW HAMPSHIRE

THE HAY ESTATE
P.O. Box 276
Newbury, NH 03255
(603) 763-4789

NEW JERSEY

LEONARD J. BUCK GARDEN
Somerset County Park
R.D. 2 Layton Road
Far Hills, NJ 07931
(201) 234-2677

BAILEY ARBORETUM
Bayville Road
Locust Valley, NY 11560
(516) 676-4487

BROOKLYN BOTANIC GARDEN
1000 Washington Avenue
Brooklyn, NY 11225
(718) 622-4433

CORNELL PLANTATIONS
One Plantations Road
Ithaca, NY 14850
(607) 255-3020

CUTLER BOTANIC GARDEN
840 Front Street
Binghamton, NY 13905
(607) 772-8953

GEORGE LANDIS ARBORETUM
Box 186, Lape Road
Espernace, NY 12066
(518) 875-6935

MOHONK MOUNTAIN HOUSE Lake Mohonk
New Paltz, NY 12561
(516) 255-1000

THE NEW YORK BOTANICAL GARDEN
T. H. Everett Memorial
Rock Garden
200th Street and
Southern Boulevard
Bronx, NY 10458-5126
(718) 817-8700

STONECROP, GARDENS INC.
RR#2, Box 371
Cold Spring, NY 10516
(914) 264-1000

UNIVERSITY BOTANICAL GARDENS AT ASHEVILLE
W.T. Weaver Boulevard
Asheville, NC 28804
(704) 252-5190

COX ARBORETUM
6733 Springboro Pike
Dayton, Ohio 45449
(513) 434-9005

BERRY BOTANIC GARDEN
11505 S.W. Summerville Avenue
Portland, OR 97219
(503) 636-4112

SHELBURNE MUSEUM & HERITAGE PARK
Route 7
Shelburne, VT 05482
(802) 985-3344

OHME GARDENS
3327 Ohme Road
Wenatchee, WA 98801
(509) 662-5785

RHODODENDRON SPECIES FOUNDATION
Weyerhauser Corporation
P.O. Box 3798
Federal Way, WA 98063
(206) 661-9377

BOERNER BOTANIC GARDENS IN WHITNELL PARK
5879 South 92nd Street
Hales Corners, WI 53130
(414) 425-1130 or 529-1870

OLBRICH BOTANICAL GARDENS
3330 Atwood Avenue
Madison, WI 53704
(608) 246-4551

MONTREAL BOTANICAL GARDEN
4101 Sherbrooke East
Montreal, Quebec H1X 2B2
(514) 872-1440

UNIVERSITY OF BRITISH COLUMBIA BOTANIC GARDEN E. H. Lohbrunner
Alpine Garden
6804 S.W. Marine Drive
Vancouver, BC V6T 1W5
(604) 228-4186

Bacon, Lionel. *Alpines*. Newton Abbot, Devon: David E. Charles Ltd., 1973.

Beckett, Kenneth, ed. *Encyclopaedia of Alpines,* Vol. 1 and 2. Avon Bank, Worcester: AGS Publications, 1993.

Bird, Richard. *A Guide to Rock Gardening*. London: Christopher Helm, 1990.

Bird, Richard, and John Kelly. *The Complete Book of Alpine Gardening*. London: Ward Lock Ltd., 1992.

Carl, Joachim; translated by Martin Kral. *Miniature Gardens,* 2nd ed. Portland, Ore.: Timber Press, 1990.

Charlesworth, Geoffrey. *The Opinionated Gardener*. Boston: David R. Godine Publisher, Inc., 1988.

––––––. *The Gardener Obsessed*. Boston: David R. Godine Publisher, Inc., 1994.

Clay, Sampson. *The Present Day Rock Garden*. London: T.C & E.C. Jack Ltd., 1937.

Deno, Norman. *Seed Germination Theory and Practice,* 2nd ed. N. Deno, 139 Lenor Dr., State College, Penn. 16801, 1993.

Elliott, Jack. *Alpines in the Open Garden*. Portland, Ore.: Timber Press, 1991.

Farrer, Reginald. *The English Rock Garden,* Vol. 1 and 2. London: T.C. & E.C. Jack Ltd., 1919.

––––––. *My Rock Garden*. London: Edward Arnold & Co., 1909.

––––––. *The Rock Garden*. London: T. Nelson & Sons Ltd., 1912.

Foerster, Karl; Kenneth A. Beckett, ed. *Rock Gardens Through the Year*. New York: Sterling Pub. Co., 1987.

Foster, H. Lincoln. *Rock Gardening*. Portland, Ore.: Timber Press, 1982 (reprint).

Foster, H. Lincoln, and Laura Louise Foster; Norman Singer, ed. *Cuttings from a Rock Garden*. New York: Atlantic Monthly Press, 1990.

Grey-Wilson, Christopher, ed. *A Manual of Alpine and Rock Garden Plants*. Portland, Ore.: Timber Press, 1989.

Griffith, Anna N. *A Guide to Rock Garden Plants*. New York: E. P. Dutton & Co., 1965.

Halliwell, Brian. *The Propagation of Alpine Plants and Dwarf Bulbs*. Portland, Ore.: Timber Press, 1992.

Harkness, Mabel G., and Deborah D'Angelo. *The Bernard E. Harkness Seedlist Handbook.* Portland, Ore.: Timber Press, 1986.

Heath, Royton E. *Collectors' Alpines,* 2nd ed. Portland, Ore.: Timber Press, 1983.

———. *Rock Plants for Small Gardens,* 3rd ed. London: Collingridge Books, 1982.

Hills, Lawrence D. *The Propagation of Alpines.* Little Compton, R.I.: Theophrastus Pub., 1976 (reprint).

Ingwersen, Will. *Alpine and Rock Plants.* London: J. M. Dent & Sons Ltd., 1983.

———. *Alpines.* Portland, Ore.: Timber Press, 1991.

———. *Ingwersen's Manual of Alpine Plants,* 2nd ed. Portland, Ore.: Timber Press, 1982.

Klaber, Doretta. *Rock Garden Plants.* New York: Bramhall House, 1959.

Kolega, Walter. *All About Rock Gardens and Plants.* New York: Doubleday & Co., 1966.

Lawrence, Elizabeth; Nancy Goodwin with Allen Lacey, eds. *A Rock Garden in the South.* Durham, N.C.: Duke University Press, 1990.

Lowe, Duncan. *Growing Alpines in Raised Beds, Troughs and Tufa.* London: B. T. Batsford Ltd., 1991.

North American Rock Garden Society. *Rock Garden Plants of North America.* Portland, Ore.: Timber Press, 1996.

Rolfe, Robert. *The Alpine House, Its Plants and Purposes.* Portland, Ore.: Timber Press, 1990.

Schacht, Wilhelm; Jim Archibald, ed. *Rock Gardens.* New York: Universe Books, 1981.

Symons-Jeune, B. H. B. *Natural Rock Gardening,* 3rd ed. London: Country Life Ltd., 1955.

Thomas, Graham Stuart. *The Rock Garden and Its Plants.* Portland, Ore.: Timber Press, 1989.

Titchmarsh, Alan. *The Rock Gardener's Handbook.* London: Croom Helm Ltd., 1983.

Wilder, Louise Beebe. *Adventures in My Garden and Rock Garden.* New York: Doubleday, Page & Co., 1926.

———. *Pleasures and Problems of a Rock Garden.* New York: Garden City Pub. Co., 1937.

Williams, Jean, ed., et al. *Rocky Mountain Alpines.* Portland, Ore.: Timber Press, 1986.